Number 118
Summer 2008

New Directions for Evaluation

Sandra Mathison
Editor-in-Chief

Reforming the Evaluation of Research

Chris L. S. Coryn
Michael Scriven
Editors

REFORMING THE EVALUATION OF RESEARCH
Chris L. S. Coryn, Michael Scriven (eds.)
New Directions for Evaluation, no. 118
Sandra Mathison, Editor-in-Chief

Microfilm copies of issues and articles are available in 16mm and 35mm, as well as microfiche in 105mm, through University Microfilms Inc., 300 North Zeeb Road, Ann Arbor, Michigan 48106-1346.

New Directions for Evaluation is indexed in Cambridge Scientific Abstracts (CSA/CIG), Contents Pages in Education (T & F), Educational Research Abstracts Online (T & F), ERIC Database (Education Resources Information Center), Higher Education Abstracts (Claremont Graduate University), Social Services Abstracts (CSA/CIG), Sociological Abstracts (CSA/CIG), and Worldwide Political Sciences Abstracts (CSA/CIG).

NEW DIRECTIONS FOR EVALUATION (ISSN 1097-6736, electronic ISSN 1534-875X) is part of The Jossey-Bass Education Series and is published quarterly by Wiley Subscription Services, Inc., A Wiley Company, at Jossey-Bass, 989 Market Street, San Francisco, California 94103-1741.

SUBSCRIPTIONS cost $85 for U.S./Canada/Mexico; $109 international. For institutions, agencies, and libraries, $215 U.S.; $255 Canada/Mexico; $289 international. Prices subject to change.

EDITORIAL CORRESPONDENCE should be addressed to the Editor-in-Chief, Sandra Mathison, University of British Columbia, 2125 Main Mall, Vancouver, BC V6T 1Z4, Canada.

www.josseybass.com

Editorial Policy and Procedures

New Directions for Evaluation, a quarterly sourcebook, is an official publication of the American Evaluation Association. The journal publishes empirical, methodological, and theoretical works on all aspects of evaluation. A reflective approach to evaluation is an essential strand to be woven through every volume. The editors encourage volumes that have one of three foci: (1) craft volumes that present approaches, methods, or techniques that can be applied in evaluation practice, such as the use of templates, case studies, or survey research; (2) professional issue volumes that present issues of import for the field of evaluation, such as utilization of evaluation or locus of evaluation capacity; (3) societal issue volumes that draw out the implications of intellectual, social, or cultural developments for the field of evaluation, such as the women's movement, communitarianism, or multiculturalism. A wide range of substantive domains is appropriate for *New Directions for Evaluation;* however, the domains must be of interest to a large audience within the field of evaluation. We encourage a diversity of perspectives and experiences within each volume, as well as creative bridges between evaluation and other sectors of our collective lives.

The editors do not consider or publish unsolicited single manuscripts. Each issue of the journal is devoted to a single topic, with contributions solicited, organized, reviewed, and edited by a guest editor. Issues may take any of several forms, such as a series of related chapters, a debate, or a long article followed by brief critical commentaries. In all cases, the proposals must follow a specific format, which can be obtained from the editor-in-chief. These proposals are sent to members of the editorial board and to relevant substantive experts for peer review. The process may result in acceptance, a recommendation to revise and resubmit, or rejection. However, the editors are committed to working constructively with potential guest editors to help them develop acceptable proposals.

Sandra Mathison, Editor-in-Chief
University of British Columbia
2125 Main Mall
Vancouver, BC V6T 1Z4
CANADA
e-mail: nde@eval.org

CONTENTS

EDITORS' NOTES

The evaluation of scientific research already has an extensive and well-structured literature on its objects, motives, methods and procedures, criteria and standards, difficulties, and results (OECD, 1997). It hardly needs elaborate philosophical underpinnings because there is normally, though not always, a consensus around what is truly important and valuable research. Simultaneously, most governments around the world recognize that current methods for evaluating research *for funding purposes* are not sufficient for current needs, and they are now funding efforts to find new and improved methods (Coryn, 2007). In the United States alone, as evidenced by the concerns of the American Council on Competitiveness, the initiative of the White House Office of Science and Technology Policy, and the National Science Foundation's funding of studies to build a science of science and innovation policy, a primary interest is assessment to understand how to improve research so that it can effectively contribute to national goals (Lal, 2006). Similar efforts exist throughout Europe, in Japan, and in Korea. Devoted to reforming evaluation of research, this volume is intended to contribute to the process of addressing this analytical need. It represents the thinking and work of some of the world's leading scholars and practitioners who are committed to improving how research is evaluated. Without staking any great claim about reforming research itself—a field of action that has rarely been out of the public eye—ultimately the suggestions here should indirectly result in increasing the quality of, and payoff from, research that is done, reducing the cost of doing it, and lending public credibility to the manner in which research is funded (Coryn, Hattie, Scriven, & Hartmann, 2007; Scriven, 2006).

In the past few decades, two major modes of assessment have dominated evaluation of scientific research: peer review, and bibliometrics (a branch of scientometrics and information science). Of the two, the former is primarily a qualitative endeavor (that is, scientific opinion), whereas the latter is mostly quantitative (objective, quantifiable indicators). Examples of other widely used approaches are (social) network analysis, case studies, tracer methodologies, spillover analysis, data mining and visualization, surveying, and econometric and other statistical modeling techniques (Ruegg & Feller, 2002; Ruegg & Jordan, 2007). Not surprisingly, the focus of the current debate has been mostly on what method to use (Julnes & Rog, 2007).

Peer review is almost universally the predominant method used for evaluating research. By and large, it is seen as an obligatory system within the scientific community and widely perceived as the only legitimate

method for valuing scientific merit. It is premised on the assumption that the quality of scientific research is an expert evaluation that can be made only by those who are extremely knowledgeable. Formalized peer review systems can be traced back to the appearance of the first scientific journals in the 17th century; yet as a cornerstone of modern scientific method, peer review has been consistently applied only since the middle of the 20th century. Although the mechanics of peer review are familiar in general terms, they are also complex and idiosyncratic. Traditionally, peer review has been a process used to evaluate individual researchers or research products for decisions about employment, promotion, publication, awards (for example, the Nobel Prize), and funding of research projects. However, in the last few decades, wide-scale use of peer panels has become commonplace to evaluate larger units, such as research groups, institutes, and research programs, and sometimes even entire scientific disciplines in order to allocate resources and set research policy priorities. In addition to scientific merit, these large-scale panels are often concerned with the socioeconomic impact of research, use of research results, or even the working conditions of researchers, among other matters. It, therefore, seems best to reserve the term *peer review* for the more traditional review and assessment systems of scholarly communities, such as reviews of manuscripts for journals, of applications for academic positions, and of grant applications. The term *expert panel evaluation* can then be used for evaluations of research that go beyond the merit of individual instances or pieces of research, or of individual researchers.

There are two subspecies of expert panel evaluation: peer panel evaluation and mixed panel evaluation (Langfeldt, 2002). One or the other is commissioned, often ad hoc, for evaluation at the program, institutional, or discipline level. Peer panel evaluation uses only researchers qualified in the subject-matter area under review. When the expert panel evaluation consists of both peers and other experts (for instance, experts on policy or commercialization of research), it is referred to as mixed panel evaluation.

With the exception of the work of Cole and Cole (1973, 1981), Chubin and Hackett (1990), Campanario (1993, 1996, 1998), and more recently Langfeldt (2002, 2006), few rigorous studies examining the workings of peer review have been undertaken, despite its importance as the basic mechanism for judging the merits of most research. To date, the most complete and critical analysis of the peer review system has been that of Cicchetti's review (1991) of its reliability. Perhaps surprisingly, he found that the reliability of most reviews is no better than would have occurred by chance. The greater part of the literature focusing on peer review consists of reports from individuals who have somehow experienced problems with the system, rather than substantive studies of it (Foltz, 2000). This is especially unfortunate; peer review often takes place at both ends of the research process and is, therefore, doubly dependent on it. First, peer review is used to assess the intellectual merits and the potential value of proposed research in order to determine whether it is worthy of funding. Second, it is often used to assess the merits of completed research for publication in scholarly journals or for citation in learned reports.

Bibliometrics is the quantitative counterpart to peer review. Modern bibliometric techniques are largely based on the work of Derek de Solla Price and Eugene Garfield. Although Garfield is usually credited as the father of bibliometrics, with the creation the Science Citation Index (SCI) at the Institute for Scientific Information (ISI) in 1961 some of its earliest applications can be traced to the second half of the 19th century, when Frank Shepard created a citation index (known as Shepard's Citations) covering judicial decisions for attorneys to use in determining whether a legal procedure was still valid (Coryn, 2007). The SCI database was originally developed for information retrieval purposes, much like Shepard's Citations, to aid researchers in locating papers of interest in the vast research literature archives. As a subsidiary function, however, it enabled scientific literature to be analyzed quantitatively and has since become a mainstay for evaluating scientific research along with the widely used impact factor, the widely debated *h*-index (Hirsh, 2005), and other citation metrics. Bibliometrics and bibliometric indicators are based on the published literature in all of its forms, including, but not limited to, journal articles, monographs, books, book chapters, conference papers and proceedings, patents, and the references they contain (Aksnes, 2005). These can be further divided into three subclasses: publication, citation, and structural indicators (Research Evaluation and Policy Project, 2005). Publication indicators include simple counts of publications and are usually viewed as a measure of research productivity, or quantity, rather than quality (Coryn, 2006). Citation indicators are the references to earlier contributions on which a scientific work was built, and against which it positions itself. They operate on the assumption that the number of citations can be regarded as a measure of scientific quality or impact (Aksnes, 2005; Moed, 2005). Structural indicators are auxiliary or proxy measures, which present information about the characteristics of research undertaken, such as publication strategies or the place of a researcher or research unit in the scientific community, and are not normally considered indicators of research performance.

Each method has its own strengths and weaknesses. However, detailed discussion exceeds the scope of this volume and is widely documented elsewhere in the scientific literature (see Foltz, 2000, for highlights of the strengths and limitations of peer review; and Moed, 2005, for applications of citation analysis in research evaluation). Many of the conceptual and methodological propositions presented by the authors of the chapters in this volume are founded on one or both of these approaches.

These chapters, which we hope to be a milestone for *New Directions for Evaluation* (in the array of international perspectives, and as a topic never before covered in the journal), offer powerful and promising insights for those working in the field of research evaluation, scientists and scholars who have been, or will be, subjected to assessment of their research, research managers, and policy makers. Regretfully, because of space limitations many fine, high-quality papers had to be left out of this volume—including contributions from Austrian, German, United Kingdom, and U.S. authors. They have been published in the fall issue (vol. 4, no. 8) of the *Journal of Multi-Disciplinary Evaluation* (http://jmde.com/) as a supplement to this volume.

In the first chapter here, Gretchen B. Jordan, Jerald Hage, and Jonathon Mote of the United States present their theories-based framework and micro- and meso-level indicators for evaluating diverse portfolios of scientific work. Next, Osamu Nakamura, Osamu Nakamura, Michiko Takagi Sawada, Shin Kosaka, Masao Koyanagi, Isao Matsunaga, Koichi Mizuno, and Naoto Kobayashi present a strategic evaluation system for research and development in Japan's public research institutes, designed to evaluate and inform strategic research policy. In chapter 3, Ireland's Bride Mallon discusses a peer-review process for assessing the contribution of artifacts, such as games and software to research. Claire Donovan, from the Research Evaluation and Policy Project (REPP), discusses various issues arising from implementation of impact measurement in the case of Australia's Research Quality Framework (RQF) in chapter 4. Next, Kathleen M. Quinlan, Mary Kane, and William M. K. Trochim synthesize the literature and findings of evaluations from four large-scale, federally funded scientific research programs in the United States to identify desired outcomes of these types of research initiatives, major evaluation challenges, and methodological principles and approaches. Chapter 6, contributed by Denis O. Gray, highlights a utilization-focused framework for evaluating research that is intended to meet the needs of scientist-managers. In the volume's concluding chapter, Michael Scriven and Chris L. S. Coryn suggest some of the logical distinctions in types of evaluation that avoid oversimplified and overcomplex approaches to the evaluation of research and apply them to some of the discussions in this volume, as well as making suggestions for ways to improve standard elements in the evaluation of research and research centers.

References

Aksnes, D. W. (2005). *Citations and their use as indicators in science policy: Studies of validity and applicability issues with a particular focus on highly-cited papers.* Unpublished doctoral dissertation, University of Twente, Enschede, Netherlands.

Campanario, J. M. (1993). Consolation for the scientist: Sometimes it is hard to publish papers that are later highly-cited. *Social Studies of Science, 23*(2), 342–362.

Campanario, J. M. (1996). Have referees rejected some of the most cited articles of all time? *Journal of the American Society for Information Science, 47*(4), 302–310.

Campanario, J. M. (1998). Peer review for journals as it stands today—Part 1. *Science Communication, 19*(3), 181–211.

Chubin, D. E., & Hackett, E. J. (1990). *Peerless science: Peer review and U.S. science policy.* Albany, NY: SUNY Press.

Cicchetti, D. (1991). The reliability of peer review for manuscript and grant submissions: A cross-disciplinary investigation. *Behavioral and Brain Sciences, 14,* 119–135.

Cole, J. R., & Cole, S. (1973). *Social stratification in science.* Chicago: Chicago University Press.

Cole, J. R., & Cole, S. (1981). *Peer review in the National Science Foundation: Phase two of a study.* Washington, DC: National Academy Press.

Coryn, C. L. S. (2006). The use and abuse of citations as indicators of research quality. *Journal of MultiDisciplinary Evaluation, 3*(4), 115–120.

Coryn, C. L. S. (2007). *Evaluation of researchers and their research: Toward making the implicit explicit.* Unpublished doctoral dissertation, Western Michigan University, Kalamazoo.

Coryn, C. L. S., Hattie, J. A., Scriven, M., & Hartmann, D. J. (2007). Models and mechanisms for evaluating government-funded research: An international comparison. *American Journal of Evaluation, 28*(4), 437–457.

Foltz, F. A. (2000). The ups and downs of peer review: Making funding choices for science. *Bulletin of Science, Technology & Society, 20*(6), 427–440.

Hirsch, J. E. (2005). An index to quantify an individual's scientific output. *ArXiv:physics/0508025.* Retrieved February 10, 2006, from http://arxiv.org/PS_cache/physics/pdf/0508/0508025v5.pdf.

Julnes, G., & Rog, D. L. (Eds.). (2007). Informing federal policies on evaluation methodology: Building the evidence base for method choice in government sponsored evaluation. *New Directions for Evaluation,* no. 113.

Lal, B. (2006, November). *Are we there yet? A review of the "social science of science policy."* Paper presented at meeting of American Evaluation Association, Portland, OR.

Langfeldt, L. (2002). *Decision-making in expert panels evaluating research: Constraints, processes and bias.* Doctoral dissertation, University of Oslo, Norway. ISBN 82-7218-465-6.

Langfeldt, L. (2006). The policy challenges of peer review: Managing bias, conflict of interests, and interdisciplinary assessments. *Research Evaluation, 15*(1), 31–41.

Moed, H. F. (2005). *Citation analysis in research evaluation.* Dordrecht, Netherlands: Springer.

OECD. (1997). *The evaluation of scientific research: Selected experiences.* Paris: Organisation for Economic Co-Operation and Development.

Research Evaluation and Policy Project. (2005). *Quantitative indicators for research assessment—A literature review.* Canberra: Australian National University, Research School and Social Sciences, Research Evaluation and Policy Project.

Ruegg, R., & Feller, I. (Eds.). (2002). *A toolkit for evaluating public R&D investment: Models, methods, and findings from ATP's first decade.* Washington, DC: U.S. Department of Commerce, Technology Administration, National Institute of Standards and Technology.

Ruegg, R., & Jordan, G. (2007). *Overview of evaluation methods for R&D programs: A directory of evaluation methods relevant to technology development programs.* Washington, DC: U.S. Department of Energy, Office of Energy Efficiency and Renewable Energy.

Scriven, M. (2006). The evaluation of research merit versus evaluation of funding of research. *Journal of MultiDisciplinary Evaluation, 3*(5), 120–123.

Chris L. S. Coryn
Michael Scriven
Editors

CHRIS L. S. CORYN *is an assistant professor and director of the Interdisciplinary Ph.D. Program in Evaluation at The Evaluation Center, Western Michigan University.*

MICHAEL SCRIVEN *is a professor of psychology teaching evaluation in the School of Behavioral and Organizational Sciences, Claremont Graduate University.*

Jordan, G. B., Hage, J., & Mote, J. (2008). A theories-based systemic framework for evaluating diverse portfolios of scientific work, part 1: Micro and meso indicators. In C. L. S. Coryn & M. Scriven (Eds.), *Reforming the evaluation of research. New Directions for Evaluation, 118,* 7–24.

1

A Theories-Based Systemic Framework for Evaluating Diverse Portfolios of Scientific Work, Part 1: Micro and Meso Indicators

Gretchen B. Jordan, Jerald Hage, Jonathon Mote

Abstract

Recently, several articles have argued for changes in the kinds of evaluation being conducted for research, technology, and development (RTD) programs. Among other suggestions, these are of special merit: (1) a more macro and systemic focus, (2) concentrating on the processes of generating innovation, (3) using theory to guide the RTD evaluation, and (4) identifying blockages and obstacles. The authors put forth a multilevel, theories-based framework of indicators for RTD evaluations that addresses these suggestions and is a guide for policy makers in policy formulation and reformulation. © Wiley Periodicals, Inc.

Note: The work presented here was completed for the Office of Basic Energy Sciences in the U.S. Department of Energy Office of Science by Sandia National Laboratories, Albuquerque, New Mexico, under contract DE-AC04–94AL8500. Sandia is operated by Sandia Corporation, a subsidiary of Lockheed Martin. Opinions expressed are solely those of the authors.

Recently, several articles (Arnold, 2004; Molas-Gallart & Davies, 2006) have appeared arguing for changes in the kinds of evaluation being made of research, technology, and development (RTD) programs. Among other suggestions, four seem to be of special merit: (1) a more macro and systemic focus, (2) greater concentration on the processes of generating innovation, (3) using theory to guide the RTD evaluation, and (4) identifying blockages and obstacles or what Arnold (2004) labels "failures." To this list of suggested changes, we would add that RTD evaluations must investigate key indicators to generate data that policy makers need in order to know what policy reformulations should be made and how.

These recent concerns about the structure of evaluations stem from a number of challenges that governments face today. In particular, we argue that three primary factors—the rising level of RTD expenditure in real terms, the importance of innovation for both economic and noneconomic goals, and the increasing speed of development of innovative solutions— significantly increase the need for evaluations that better guide government policy formation and reformulation.

The objective of this chapter is to outline a theories-based innovation systems framework (ISF) of indicators for RTD evaluations that can aid government policy makers in policy formulation and reformulation. The indicators that are proposed suggest protocols for performance monitoring and evaluation; they could form the basis of a new kind of data structure for science reporting agencies, such as the National Science Foundation (NSF). Although the ISF we have developed is multilevel in nature, this chapter focuses on the micro- and meso-analytical levels. We address the issue of macro indicators and their relationship to the micro and meso elsewhere (Hage, Jordan, & Mote, 2007). The systemic framework we suggest has significant potential for developing socioeconometric models that incorporate the innovation processes necessary for predicting innovation outcomes (or throughput), a request recently made by John Marburger (2005), the director of the U.S. Office of Science and Technology Policy.

Central to this is the idea innovation network theory (Hage & Hollingsworth, 2000), which describes the innovation processes and identifies a number of potential blockages in the connectedness of innovation networks in technology sectors or regimes. The theory argues that there are six research arenas in the process of innovation (basic, applied, development, manufacturing, quality, and commercialization research) and strong linkages among these arenas are critical for continued innovation. In our framework, the meso level connects to the micro level that encompasses Jordan's theory of research profiles (2006) and previous work on industrial innovation (Hage, 1999), and it offers a larger context for discussing potential organizational obstacles to innovation. The meso level permits focus when connecting to the macro level, encompassing the various institutional theories in the national system of innovation literature (Hall & Soskice, 2001; Nelson, 1993) and the new work on institutional change (Campbell, 2004), as well as permitting discussions of obstacles to innovation created by various institutional rules.

Together, the three levels answer a plea for a theory of knowledge production that contains these three analytical levels (Hage & Meeus, 2006) and creates an opportunity for contributing to other theories and frameworks, such as organizational learning and knowledge communities, and for putting the throughput or black box of RTD into standard econometric input-output evaluation models.

Within each analytical level, we identify three sets of indicators that provide guidance for policy makers, as well as indicate specific possible blockages and obstacles. In general, micro indicators focus on how to allocate funds using the criteria of balanced investments (public-private) across the six RTD arenas in a technological sector, across the portfolio of investments within each arena, and across selected research organizations with the appropriate organizational profiles for the portfolio choices. Similarly, meso-level indicators measure the outputs of each arena in real time, the strength of the connectedness between differentiated arenas, and the overall assessment of innovation performance including societal impact.

A Theories-Led Innovation Systems Framework for RTD Evaluation

As Weiss (1997) discusses, a theory-based evaluation allows one to address the most relevant mechanisms that mediate between processes and outcomes and better understand how programs work. A particularly useful way of capturing the complexity of the innovation process from scientific advance to socioeconomic outcomes is contained in the idea innovation network theory of Hage and Hollingsworth (2000). The idea innovation network theory starts with a simple idea, namely that in many technological sectors (especially the more high-tech ones), commercially viable product innovations necessitate research in the six arenas diagrammed in Figure 1.1. The theory builds on the conceptual nonlinear model of Kline and Rosenberg (1986) but alters the focus to arenas within a technological sector, and adds the concept of quality research to the original five areas.

Why be concerned about all six arenas in the innovation process? The process of generating scientific advance and innovation in products or processes that have socioeconomic impact can be thought of as "throughput." The idea innovation network theory presents a necessarily complex view of the throughput of the innovation process and does so at the meso-technological-sector level, where indicators and socioeconometric models of innovative performance can be constructed. Another advantage of this theory is that it can expose research "gaps." Some of these arenas have been ignored, with detrimental consequences for the competitive position of certain countries. These arenas include quality-control research in the sense of fewer defects and lower operating costs, but also research that reduces the

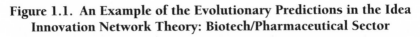

Figure 1.1. An Example of the Evolutionary Predictions in the Idea Innovation Network Theory: Biotech/Pharmaceutical Sector

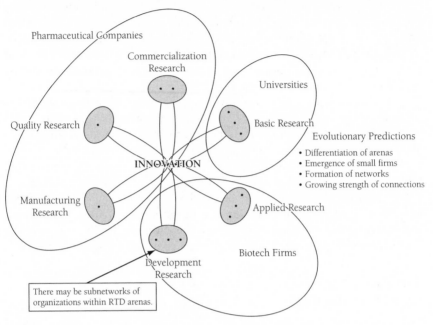

various externalities of the products, such as energy consumption, global warming, and health risks. The importance stems from three considerations: (1) reducing costs, and potentially, the export of jobs to developing countries, (2) increasing customization so that multiple products can be produced on the same assembly line, and (3) reducing externalities.

Consistent with Kline and Rosenberg (1986), a good idea for an innovative product or service can start in any one of these six arenas. The process of innovation is nonlinear, with ideas moving back and forth between arenas multiple times; hence, the use of the word *network* rather than chain. The real meaning of the term *network* is the argument that each of these arenas must be connected, and if one of the arenas has a radical advance in knowledge, it must be strongly connected to the other arenas for transfer of the tacit knowledge involved in the radical knowledge advance. Strong connections are defined as face-to-face interactions with frequent meetings. Without these strong connections, then the radical advance in knowledge is not likely to be exploited in a timely fashion.

Analytical Focus at the Meso Level. The analytical focus of the ISF is the meso level of the technological sector, which others have also identified as critical (Archibugi & Pianta, 1992; Guerrieri & Tylecote, 1997; Malerba & Orsenigo, 1993, 1996; Pavitt, 1984). This meso level of arenas and networks is ideal for allowing one to connect to the macro institutional level of the national system of innovation and to the micro research organizations that are its constituent parts, thus also providing the often overlooked linkage between the micro and macro levels. This is important because the average scale of the research projects often varies; so, too, the rate of technological change and the pace of product innovation typically vary from one sector to another. For example, some sectors, such as semiconductors, see radical breakthroughs in the performance characteristics of chips every 18 months. In contrast, sectors such as pharmaceuticals have a much slower pace, despite a higher level of RTD investment. Finally, policy makers are usually interested in intervening at the technological sector level to achieve their various goals. Hence, the meso level is an advantageous starting point for development of a set of key indicators for an evaluation framework, rather than the national system of innovation as the analytical focus. Further, because the meso level in this framework is connected to the macro level, it does not mean that one is ignoring this aspect of the innovation process.

An Overview of the Scheme of Indicators. A schematic of the general argument in the framework of indicators is in Figure 1.2. At each level—the micro, the meso, and the macro—we have chosen three sets of indicators. The three sets of indicators at each level permit better appreciation of how policies affect particular arenas of the idea innovation network as well as their connections and thus can lead to more fine tuning of these policies. With this information, policy makers can assess what they have accomplished so far and then decide where they want to be in the next five to ten years. Best of all, evaluations with these sets of indicators at each analytical level are more likely to aid identification of the obstacles or bottlenecks (Arnold, 2004). Indeed, intervention may be essential if the mission goals of the policy makers are to be achieved; thus, this aspect of the framework—clearly identifying organizational, network, and institutional failures—is critical. With this perspective, the evaluator can shift from simply measuring "what is done" or accomplished to identifying "what could be."

The Micro Level of Indicators: Balanced Investments in Arenas, Portfolios, and Organizational Profiles

At the micro level, evaluators need to be concerned about three key sets of indicators in order to assess and develop good policy guidelines for interventions. These three sets of indicators focus on aspects of the first and most common form of government intervention, allocation of research funds. Usually, when governments decide to achieve a mission such as national security or become more competitive, they begin by increasing RTD spending. Before governments allocate more money, there should be an assessment of how the money (both public and private) is presently being spent and whether or not there are research gaps.

Figure 1.2. The Innovation Systems Framework for RTD Evaluations

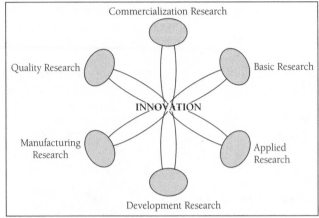

• High-risk capital—available where?
• Capabilities—level, mix, availability?
• Modes of coordination—effective?

Macro: Institutional rules as they affect the sector

Commercialization Research

Quality Research

Basic Research

Meso: Performance by sectors and arena

INNOVATION

• Socioeconomic outcomes
• Technical progress
• Network connectedness

Manufacturing Research

Applied Research

Development Research

Micro: Funds allocation by arena and profile

• RTD arenas—are there sufficient funds?
• Portfolios—need more/less radical, large scope?
• Organizational profiles—do attributes match the profile?

The idea innovation network immediately focuses attention on the amount of investment in *each* of the six arenas and helps locate potential gaps blocking achievement of the desired throughput. Recognizing the complexity of the innovation processes also alters how one regards disbursement of RTD funds to portfolio choices, classified by the degree of radicalness and the scope of focus. Every strategic choice of incremental versus radical and narrow scope versus broad scope must be evaluated in each of the six arenas. By the same logic, this should result in reconsideration of how funds are allocated to projects and research organizations to have the desired fit between strategy and organization profile (Jordan, 2006). Further, one can begin to assess whether organizational blockages are part of the reason for lack of technical progress in the strategic choices that the RTD government has made.

Balanced Investments Across Six Arenas. We must begin with the objectives of government policy makers, with the critical issues being the desired aims (innovation) and identification of the most appropriate technological sector(s) to pursue these innovations. For example, the EU has recently decided to emphasize the technological sectors of health, pharmaceuticals, energy, environment, security, electronic equipment, and transport and logistics. Given the choice of these sectors for stimulating innovation, the policy maker or evaluator needs to determine the amount of RTD spending in each of the six arenas, including both public and private expenditures, in a sector. One issue for the assessment to determine is whether one or two of these arenas are being ignored or underfunded. Many U.S. products have lacked the quality necessary to compete in a global market, which suggests a lack of funding at least by the private sector in this arena.

Some might question the necessity of funding RTD in all six arenas. The importance of research in all six arenas is highlighted in what are typically referred to as the high-tech sectors in the United States. In these sectors, radical product innovations usually require radical advances in knowledge in more than one arena. Consider the case of semiconductors and Moore's law, which not only reflects radical advances in performance characteristics of the product, but also necessitates radical advances in knowledge about how to manufacture the new generation of chips and how to achieve quality control. It could be the science is already in place, but there is a need for some radical advances in one or two other arenas.

One of the advantages of this systemic framework for describing the complex processes of innovation is that it broadens our concept about the types of innovation beyond the usual distinctions. Product and process (manufacturing) innovation have been joined to research about commercialization and quality control, including development of new qualities. More important, the two forms of scientific research, basic and applied, are united with industrial innovation, a connection that has been underemphasized (Jordan, 2006). The key point is that a radical new product might develop out of any one or two of these arenas. Thus, the word *balance* means assessing what is the appropriate amount for each arena. Although ideas move back and forth in the idea innovation network, the research problems in the several arenas, which, in turn, necessitate increases in expenditure, occur across time.

Usually within a technological sector, the expensive unsolved problems for research are quite well understood and can be isolated in a specific arena. In pharmaceutical research, for example, clinical trials are expensive and yet are fundamental for successful commercialization of a new drug. In automobiles, it is more likely to be engineering research for product development, whereas in aircraft research the need for applied research on fuel-efficient engines and lightweight materials for the body of the aircraft are perennial research questions. Because this framework has not been used extensively and there is a tendency to focus primarily on basic, applied, and product development research, norms about the ideal amounts do not currently exist.

Distribution of Projects by Portfolio Within the Six Arenas. Governments choose missions, and the question is not just how much to spend, but whether these missions require radical solutions or solutions that necessitate a broad-scope focus. To take a European example, when France decided to develop high-speed trains, it had to redesign everything, including ticket sales. This means radical advances in basic research, applied research, product development, manufacturing, quality control, and commercialization research. Reporting the distribution of RTD expenditures must start with the basic question of the aims of that funding; that is, how radical an advance does the government desire in the specific technological sector being assessed? This leads naturally into another way of describing research gaps: by the distribution of spending in the portfolio.

What are some standard ways for describing portfolios? The two basic strategic choices are relative emphasis on incremental versus radical breakthrough or high-risk research, and relative emphasis on many projects with narrow scope versus a few broad-scoped programs (Jordan, 2006). Practically, we are suggesting that the amount of money, both public and private, spent in these four categories should be assessed within each arena. For example, the U.S. government would like to have radically new technologies to reduce dependence on oil. Given this, one examines the portfolio of projects in the various energy sectors associated with alternative energies and determines the relative emphasis on radical advances and broad-scope projects designed to reduce dependence on oil.

Given a decision to develop a radical product or service, the problem is then to determine which arenas should have the radical advances in knowledge. This can vary with the situation. To continue with the example of developing alternative energies to reduce dependence on oil, the choice of arena depends on the specific alternative. The science and technology for biofuels for automobiles has largely been developed. Here, the problem in the United States is one of commercialization research, to determine how best to secure customer interest, and creation of new distribution systems for this kind of fuel.

Likewise, certain missions necessitate a broad scope of focus for the research. The decision about the scope of the research project is more likely to be determined by the nature of the research work in one or more arenas. In the area of alternative energies, the best example is fusion power research. Inherent in the problem is the need for very expensive equipment, a relatively large number of researchers, and expanded budgets. Here, is an example of a broad scope of focus project that involves the goal of radical advances in a number of arenas, among them manufacturing (reduce the cost of cooling), quality (reducing the risk of explosion), and commercialization (how to win acceptance of nuclear energy).

In this manner, an assessment would report the distribution of RTD funds, both public and private, in each of the six arenas in four possible kinds of research projects in a portfolio:

1. Narrow scope of focus and incremental advances
2. Narrow scope of focus and radical advances
3. Broad scope of focus and incremental advances
4. Broad scope of focus and radical advances

Figure 1.3. Dimensions of Strategy and Structure Define Four Research Profiles

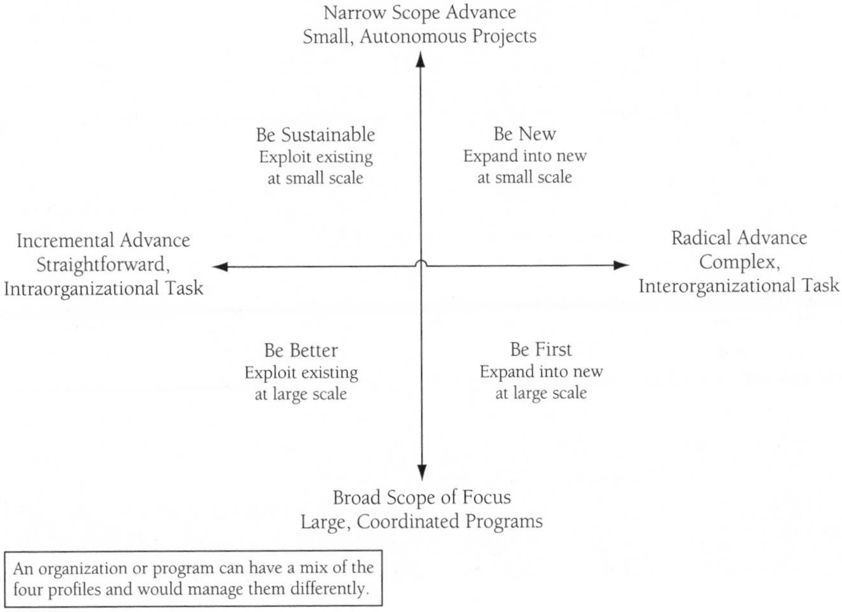

Narrow Scope Advance
Small, Autonomous Projects

Be Sustainable
Exploit existing
at small scale

Be New
Expand into new
at small scale

Incremental Advance
Straightforward,
Intraorganizational Task

Radical Advance
Complex,
Interorganizational Task

Be Better
Exploit existing
at large scale

Be First
Expand into new
at large scale

Broad Scope of Focus
Large, Coordinated Programs

An organization or program can have a mix of the four profiles and would manage them differently.

Figure 1.3 describes the four kinds of research projects. It is entirely possible that an arena would have a mixture of them, depending on the nature of the problem and the objectives of the government.

The Distribution of Projects by Organizational Profile Attributes. The third set of indicators for evaluation at the micro level represents an inventory of the number of research organizations and projects within each arena of the technological sector that have appropriate characteristics for achieving the research objectives in a chosen portfolio. Rather than just report the number of research organizations, which is the typical approach, our framework focuses attention on the number of research projects and organizations with particular attributes and characteristics. These characteristics are listed in Table 1.1 (see Jordan, 2005; and Jordan, Streit, & Binkley, 2003). As one can observe, there are familiar themes of the organic organization, complexity or diversity in division of labor, leaders with vision, and, of course, resources. The characteristics reflect organizations handling of tensions between flexibility and coordination and between interorganizational collaborations and organizational control, to name two.

Assessment of the research environments would then report how many projects have the characteristics associated with the attributes related to radical advances in knowledge and how many have the characteristics associated with broad scope of focus, and, of course, both. In each instance, the

**Table 1.1. Organizational Profile Attributes Associated
With Strategic Choices**

Process Attributes for Radicalness	*Process Attributes for Large Scope*
Encourage exploration, risk taking	Clearly define goals and strategies
• Time to think and explore	• Research vision and strategies
• Pursuit of new ideas	• Sufficient, stable funding
• Autonomy in decision making	• Investing in future capabilities
Integrate ideas, internally and externally	Plan and execute well
• Internal cross-fertilization of ideas	• Project planning and execution
• External collaborations and interactions	• Project-level measures of success
• Integrate ideas and R&D portfolios	• Labwide measures of success
Encourage change and critical thinking	Build strategic relationships
• Sense of challenge and enthusiasm	• Relationship with sponsors
• Commitment to critical thinking	• Champion foundational research
• Identify new projects and opportunities	• Reputation for excellence

issue is to match funding for the organizational profile to chosen strategies. Table 1.1 focuses on what might be called organizational failures, which Arnold (2004) called *institutional* failures, but which we believe should be kept quite separate from other kinds of institutional failures (those that are a consequence of institutional rules; Hage, 2006; Hage & Meeus, 2006; North, 1990).

Meso-Level Indicators: Six Arena Outputs, Network Connectedness, Overall Sector Performance

Increasing expenditures that are then allocated across the idea innovation network in accordance with strategic decisions made about the portfolio, and awarding funds to research organizations capable of performing these strategic choices, are not the only kind of policy intervention. As important is to know if the government is achieving what it desires. For example, suppose that the government has decided it wants radical innovations in a newly created set of biotech companies, as did Germany (Casper, 2006). The issue is whether these companies are, in fact, achieving radical biotech innovations. To have leading indicators for sector performance, one needs to assess the technical outputs *in real time* of each arena and the strength of the network connectedness within and between arenas, and then relate them to the overall performance of the sector.

Real-Time Technical Achievements in Each Arena. In the Hage and Hollingsworth network theory (2000), each arena is perceived to have an output. In turn, these outputs can be evaluated on the basis of how radical the advance is in that specific arena. The radical nature of the advance in the technical output is a question of the context and how a radical advance is defined. Radical advances reflect a large increase in the specific indicator defining the achievement in an output. Automation that improved the throughput of dishwashing machines by 300% clearly represented a radical advance as a consequence of manufacturing research. New paradigms or theories, though rare, are usually considered radical advances in science and are later recognized as such (as with Nobel Prizes). Where does peer review fit into this measurement framework? Peer reviewers usually have the knowledge necessary to define the typical rate of advance in an area as well as what is considered incremental and what would be a radical advance.

Some suggestions as to the kinds of measures of technical progress in output for each arena are presented in Table 1.2. The outputs have to be measured in real time—usually at least annually—for a number of reasons. A major one is to give quick feedback to policy makers. Papers and patents appear 2 to 5 years after completion of a project in many cases; citations unfold even more slowly. A second reason is that for policy or management intervention to be effective, it must occur while the project is still in progress. Although the reasons for lack of technical progress can adhere in many places in the innovation system, a good place to begin is with the management of the research project and whether the attributes appropriate for the specific strategic choices listed in Table 1.1 are present and to what degree.

A third reason to measure technical progress in each arena is to establish the links between short-term and medium- and long-term evaluations. This speaks to two problems: (1) the tenuousness of system evaluations of the medium and long run and (2) selection of quantifiable indicators that are easy to collect but deny the complexity of the innovation process and run the risk of irrelevancy. We believe Table 1.2 helps solve this problem. Beyond this, by establishing the missing link between short-term and medium- or long-term evaluations at the systemic level, one is also constructing a theory of the national system of innovation and developing a number of insights about institutional theory.

Measuring the technical achievements in the six arenas may appear to be an expensive and formidable task. Because each arena output tends to be the concern of a particular agency or ministry, the cost can be spread among them; the information about each arena individually is of value and collectively more than the simple sum of the six parts. For example, the ministry of the environment would want to know if the products are being manufactured with qualities that protect the environment in various ways; the ministry of commerce is interested in establishing new methods for advertising and distributing products; and the ministry of technology, if there is one separate from a ministry of science or industry, is more concerned with research on manufacturing and product development.

Further, Table 1.2 offers suggestions for each arena, but it may not be necessary to measure all six. This is a question of how much functional differentiation has occurred. For example, if basic, applied, and product development

Table 1.2. Indicators of Technical Output for Each Functional Arena in the Idea Innovation Network

Functional Arena	Measures of Scientific/Technical Advanced in Output
Basic research	• Percentage increase in modeling of some scientific behavior • Solution to a central problem • Identification of new concepts or processes
Applied research	• Percentage increase in control over some desired attribute
Product development or product innovation	• Percentage increase in performance characteristics weighted by their importance • Addition of new properties to the functionality of the product
Production research or process innovation	• Percentage increase in productivity • Percentage increase in customization
Quality control research and research on qualities	• Percentage decrease in defects • Percentage decrease in operating costs • Percentage decrease in various externalities weighted by their importance
Commercialization research	• Percentage increase in customer satisfaction • Percentage decrease in delivery time

research are combined in a biotech company, and if the manufacturing, quality, and marketing research are combined in a pharmaceutical firm, one can concentrate on the technical outputs of product development of the biotech companies and the product outputs of the pharmaceutical firms. This represents only a first approximation; again, it may be necessary to examine the outputs of the other arenas within the biotech companies and the pharmaceutical firms because blockage can be organizational, with bottlenecks between basic and applied research in the biotech companies or between manufacturing research and quality research in the pharmaceutical companies. For this, internal network analysis can be quite valuable (Mote, 2005).

As more and more of the arenas become functionally differentiated, one is forced to measure the technical outputs of each arena. It speaks to the issue of understanding the innovation processes at the level of the idea innovation network in a technical sector, avoiding the errors in the business systems literature and other institutional studies that tend to generalize from one technological sector to all others (Hollingsworth, 1997; Whitley, 1992a, 1992b).

The Strength of Connectedness Between Arenas. It should be clear that the six arenas of the idea innovation network need to have strong connections to have the desired result. In the past, when all arenas were within the same organization as with Siemens, DuPont, and Procter & Gamble, the issue of connectedness did not present a significant problem. However, over time, connectedness has become problematic, even within the same organization. For example, disconnectedness occurred between Bell Laboratories and AT&T and between the research department (PARC) of Xerox and the main company. The real problem starts to grow as an entire functional arena becomes disconnected; an example is all of basic research being located outside the other organizations involved in some technological sector. The van Waarden and Oosterwijk (2001) EU study indicates how these evolutionary processes have unfolded in telecommunications and pharmaceuticals in Austria, Finland, Germany, and the Netherlands. A number of new subnetworks in specific arenas emerged to handle the problems of technical advances, and, in turn, they were connected to the larger idea innovation network.

As each arena becomes differentiated into separate research organizations, concern grows as to the extent of the connection between these differentiated arenas. Even more important is the strength of the connection. Hage and Hollingsworth (2000) argue that as the radical nature of the technical achievement in a specific arena increases, the more frequent and intense must be the interaction with other arenas to transfer the tacit knowledge involved in the radical advance.

What reveals the strength of the connection? Here are some indicators: (1) transfer of people from one research group to another, both within and among organizations; (2) joint research projects involving face-to-face collaboration among researchers, as distinct from long-distance collaboration; (3) joint publications; (4) the strength of managerial, financial, and research ties among organizations in joint ventures; and (5) the strength of ties among actors in research consortia (Nieminen & Kaukonen, 1999). Van Waarden and Oosterwijk (2001) observe a large number of ways in which connectedness was established: joint ventures, user groups, product teams, patent pools, collective trademarks, technology clusters, partnerships, alliances, and even virtual firms. But it should be observed that having a number of these mechanisms present does not necessarily reflect transfer of tacit knowledge. Just as one wants to measure the knowledge advances in each arena, one also needs to measure exchanges of tacit knowledge within and between arenas, especially the differentiated ones.

The idea innovation network highlights two kinds of networks that should be of concern for policy makers, and thus evaluators, to measure: subnetworks of small research organizations within an arena, and networks of organizations (whether small or large) across differentiated arenas. The former are important when governments are interested in creating technical pools, which was clearly the objective of the U.S. government when it changed its antitrust laws to encourage research consortia. In this instance, some of the research consortia involved quite large organizations, primarily concentrated in the basic and applied arenas of research, leaving product development to individual companies that desired to pursue particular market niches. In contrast, the networks of organizations become especially important in linking differentiated arenas. But that said, the more critical point is that it is not necessary and may even be counterproductive to have networks and subnetworks everywhere.

Recently, a large number of network studies have emerged, including the new research on visualization tools that mine large data sets involving papers, patents, and citations of either papers or patents or both (Börner, Sanyal, & Vespignani, 2006; Wagner, 2005). Many of these efforts are attempts to measure the payoff from investments in RTD. However useful these network analyses are for examining the consequences of certain government policies, they are focusing on what *is* rather than what *can be*. The ISF and measurement of connectedness in real time attempts to inform government about network failures or "what could be." With policy reformulation, government could potentially achieve more payoff from its investments in science than it does presently.

Overall Performance of the Technology Sector. The technical outputs of each arena are a means to an end, locating one of the reasons a nation may not be achieving its goals. The lack of connectedness can be another reason. But in the final analysis, evaluators need to assess the overall performance of the technological sector. Rather than a single assessment of the overall performance, we suggest these dimensions:

- The degree of radicalness on the various dimensions of the product mix
- The average speed of product dimension development or time to market
- The commercial success of the product mix in sales and trade balances or the technological position globally

It goes without saying that the level of analysis here is not the single research organization, but all of those concerned with producing products in a particular technological sector and, therefore, the product mix in the technological sector. First, although we are using economic examples, we argue that the same logic can be applied to health products, military weapons, and national security. The industrial innovation literature (Hage, 1999; Hage & Meeus, 2006) has tended to focus on product innovation and even radical product innovation in terms of functionality, rather than observing that it is one of a set of interrelated dimensions. Second, consistent with the repeated importance of research on qualities, and research on customization of manufacturing, product mixes at the sector level should be evaluated along a variety of dimensions to understand correctly the competitive position of the country. Third, it is fairly easy to determine the competitive position of the product mix for policy makers using trade journals and statements of marketing executives who

are acutely aware of the relative strengths and weaknesses of their products in a global context.

Also, the average speed of development across the various dimensions
involved in the product mix has increased and become a critical factor in
maintaining a country's competitive position in the high-tech sectors. The
Japanese set the bar quite high when they created the hybrid car, a radical
product innovation, in just 15 months (Nonaka & Peltokorpi, 2006).

Conclusions

Recent calls for theory-led evaluation and better analyses of the systemic
obstacles and blockages to innovation to explain why policy objectives have
or have not been reached reflect a new era in RTD evaluation. These changes
in the methodology of evaluation focus on what could be rather than what
is done. If theory-led evaluations can determine what obstacles or blockages
are preventing realization of the objectives of policy makers, then governments could begin the process of designing better interventions to achieve
more effective innovation.

But which theory or theories should lead the evaluations? Although
some have called for use of national systems of innovation literature, this
literature is largely descriptive and covers only the macro level. We have
suggested that the systemic framework should be a theory-led evaluation, that is, include theories from the macro, meso, and micro levels.
One advantage of starting to construct the ISF with the idea innovation
network theory of Hage and Hollingsworth (2000) is that it helps integrate these other literatures at the same time that it affords a more complex perspective on the throughput of the innovation processes. Theories
from each of the three levels are essential if one is to understand the
blockages and obstacles because they could be located in any part of
the system.

Despite pleas from governments that one analyze the entire scientific
and technological system, we suggest that instead it is more desirable to
evaluate sector by sector. If need be, these separate sector analyses could be
combined into a total assessment. Another implication of the call for analysis of blockages and obstacles is that technical advances have to be measured
in real time, rather than waiting for the appearance of papers, patents, and
citations to them. If governments are ever to focus on improving policies,
they must have quick feedback, not only on whether they are failing to
achieve their objectives, but more critically on the reasons. Only then can
governments learn how to fashion policies to improve. Only then can evaluators relate short-term accomplishments to long-term sector performances.
Then, evaluations would truly inform governments and reduce the current
cynicism about evaluation that almost always states that research investments are successful.

The ISF for RTD evaluation can inform not only governments, but the theories that have been used to further construct the framework. The efficacy of various theories can be tested across the three levels of analysis (macro, meso, and micro contributions to any particular issue). Government interventions, if evaluated this way, could then supply some important answers to questions that have been imposed in these various literatures: What are the best kinds of linkage for the transfer of tacit knowledge? Can governments overcome path dependency? How much autonomy do research organizations have from their institutional environment? Answers to questions such as these would considerably advance the sophistication of social science theory.

References

Archibugi, D., & Pianta, M. (1992). *The technological specialization of advanced countries: A report to the EEC on international science and technology activities.* Boston: Kluwer.

Arnold, E. (2004). Evaluating research and innovation policy: A systems world needs systems evaluations. *Research Evaluation, 13*(1), 3–17.

Börner, K., Sanyal, S., & Vespignani, A. (2006). Network science: A theoretical and practical framework. *Annual Review of Information Science and Technology, 41,* 537–607.

Campbell, J. L. (2004). *Institutional change and globalization.* Princeton, NJ: Princeton University Press.

Casper, S. (2006). Exporting the silicon valley to Europe: How useful is comparative institutional theory? In J. Hage & M. T. H. Meeus (Eds.), *Innovation, science and institutional change: A handbook of research* (pp. 483–504). Oxford, UK: Oxford University Press.

Guerrieri, P., & Tylecote, A. (1997). Interindustry differences in technical change and national patterns of technological accumulation. In C. Edquist (Ed.), *Systems of innovation: Technologies, institutions and organizations* (pp. 107–129). London: Pinter.

Hage, J. (1999). Organizational innovation and organizational change. *Annual Review of Sociology, 25,* 597–622.

Hage, J. (2006). Introduction, part IV. In J. Hage & M. T. H. Meeus (Eds.), *Innovation, science and institutional change: A handbook of research* (pp. 415–422). Oxford, UK: Oxford University Press.

Hage, J., & Hollingsworth, J. R. (2000). A strategy for analysis of idea innovation networks and institutions. *Organizational Studies, 5,* 971–1004.

Hage, J., Jordan, G., & Mote, J. (2007). A theories-based innovation systems framework for evaluating diverse portfolios of scientific work, part two: Macro indicators and policy interventions. *Science and Public Policy, 34*(10), 731–741.

Hage, J., & Meeus, M. (2006). Product and process innovation, scientific research, knowledge dynamics, and institutional change: An introduction. In J. Hage and M. T. H. Meeus (Eds.), *Innovation, science and institutional change: A handbook of research* (pp. 1–19). Oxford, UK: Oxford University Press.

Hollingsworth, J. R. (1997). Continuities and changes in social systems of production: The cases of Japan, Germany, and the United States. In J. R. Hollingsworth & R. Boyer (Eds.), *Contemporary capitalism: The embeddedness of institutions* (pp. 256–310). New York: Cambridge University Press.

Jordan, G. (2005). What is important to R&D workers. *Research Technology Management, 48*(3), 23–32.

Jordan, G. (2006). Factors influencing advances in basic and applied research: Variation due to diversity in research profiles. In J. Hage & M. T. H. Meeus (Eds.), *Innovation, science and institutional change: A handbook of research* (pp. 173–195). Oxford, UK: Oxford University Press.

Jordan, G., Hage, J., & Mote, J. (2006, April). *A theory-based framework for evaluating diverse portfolios of scientific work.* Paper presented at the New Frontiers in Evaluation conference, Vienna, Austria.

Jordan, G., Streit, L. D., & Binkley, J. S. (2003). Assessing and improving the effectiveness of national research laboratories. *IEEE Transactions on Engineering Management, 50*(2), 228–235.

Kline, S., & Rosenberg, N. (1986). An overview of innovation. In R. Landau & N. Rosenberg (Eds.), *The positive sum strategy.* Washington, DC: National Academy Press.

Lundvall, B. A. (1992). *National systems of innovation: Towards a theory of innovation and interactive learning.* London, UK: Pinter.

Lundvall, B. A. (1993). Explaining interfirm cooperation and innovation limits of the transaction-cost approach. In G. Grabher (Ed.), *The embedded firm: On the socioeconomics of industrial networks.* London: Routledge.

Malerba, F., & Orsenigo, L. (1993). Technological regimes and firm behavior. *Industrial and Corporate Change, 2,* 45–71.

Malerba, F., & Orsenigo, L. (1996). Technological regimes and sectoral patterns of innovative activities. *Industrial and Corporate Change, 6,* 83–117.

Marburger, J. H. (2005). *Statement of Dr. John H. Marburger, III, President's Science Adviser and Director, Office of Science and Technology Policy, to the United States House of Representatives, Committee on Science, Fiscal Year 2006 Federal R&D Budget, February 16, 2005.* Retrieved June 6, 2007 from www.house.gov/science/hearings

Molas-Gallart, J., & Davies, A. (2006). Toward a theory-led evaluation: The experience of European science, technology, and innovation policies. *American Journal of Evaluation, 27*(1), 64–82.

Mote, J. E. (2005). R&D ecology: Using 2-mode network analysis to explore complexity in R&D environments. *Journal of Engineering and Technology Management, 22,* 93–111.

Nieminen, M., & Kaukonen, E. (1999). University research in innovation systems: Reflections based on the Finnish case. In G. Schienstock & O. Kuusi (Eds.), *Transformation towards a learning economy: The challenge for the Finnish innovation system.* Helsinki: SITRA.

Nelson, R. R. (Ed.). (1993). *National innovation systems: A comparative study.* Oxford, UK: Oxford University Press.

Nonaka, I., & Peltokorpi, V. (2006). Knowledge-based view of radical innovation: Toyota Prius case. In J. Hage & M. T. H. Meeus (Eds.), *Innovation, science and institutional change: A handbook of research* (pp. 88–104). Oxford, UK: Oxford University Press.

North, D. (1990). *Institutions, institutional change, and economic performance.* Cambridge, UK: Cambridge University Press.

Pavitt, K. (1984). Sectoral patterns of technical change: Towards a taxonomy and a theory. *Research Policy, 13,* 343–373.

van Waarden, F., & Oosterwijk, H. (2001). Turning tracks? Path dependence, technological paradigm shifts, and organizational and institutional change. In F. van Waarden (Ed.), *Building bridges between ideas and markets, part I: Some summary findings and part II, annex 1, country-specific reports* (Final Report of the TSER-Funded Project). Utrecht, the Netherlands: Utrecht University.

Wagner, C. (2005). Six case studies of international collaboration in science. *Scientometrics, 62*(1), 3–36.

Weiss, C. (1997). Theory-based evaluation: Past, present and future. In D. J. Rog & D. Fournier (Eds.), *Progress and future directions in evaluation: Perspectives on theory, practice, and methods. New Directions for Program Evaluation, 76,* 41–55.

Whitley, R. (1992a). *Business systems in East Asia: Firms, markets and societies*. London: Sage.

Whitley, R. (1992b). *European business systems: Firms and markets in their national contexts*. London: Sage.

GRETCHEN B. JORDAN *is a principal member of the technical staff at Sandia National Laboratories.*

JERALD HAGE *is director of the Center for Innovation, Department of Sociology, University of Maryland.*

JONATHON MOTE *is an assistant research scientist at the Center for Innovation, Department of Sociology, University of Maryland.*

NEW DIRECTIONS FOR EVALUATION • DOI: 10.1002/ev

Nakamura, O., Nakamura, O., Sawada, M. T., Kosaka, S., Koyanagi, M., Matsunaga, I., Mizuno, K., & Kobayashi, N. (2008). Strategic evaluation of research and development in Japan's public research institutes. In C. L. S. Coryn & M. Scriven (Eds.), *Reforming the evaluation of research. New Directions for Evaluation, 118,* 25–36.

2

Strategic Evaluation of Research and Development in Japan's Public Research Institutes

Osamu Nakamura, Osamu Nakamura, Michiko Takagi Sawada, Shin Kosaka, Masao Koyanagi, Isao Matsunaga, Koichi Mizuno, Naoto Kobayashi

Abstract

The authors describe a strategic evaluation system for research and development (R&D) in Japan's public research institutes, using examples implemented in the National Institute of Advanced Industrial Science and Technology (AIST). Important issues include promoting coherent and concurrent research on the basis of a strategy to bring about outcomes, and performing the evaluation from the perspective of outcomes in order to develop a clear scenario that might be related to future innovations. © Wiley Periodicals, Inc.

Public research institutes for research and development (R&D) in the field of industrial technology have a special mission to contribute to industrial transformation by developing innovative technologies. This mission differs from that of universities, which are responsible for advanced research and education, and from that of industries, whose products are used practically in society. Although the evaluation indices used by the

former tend to rely on academic research results, such as scientific papers and educational effects, and those of the latter emphasize profits in the market, it is difficult to rely on those indices for public research institutes performing R&D. Therefore, we need to design suitable and applicable evaluation systems.

Formation of a research strategy is especially important for the public research institutes. The strategy leads the individual R&D programs or projects, and the results of evaluation for these activities can, in turn, be reflected in the next stage of activities, depending on the next stage of the strategy.

We call the evaluation of strategic activities of an organization *strategic evaluation*. This includes several basic components described in the sections of this chapter. Especially important items are *evaluation from the viewpoint of outcomes*, effective reflection of the evaluation, and linkage of evaluation to layers of the organizations involved.

In this chapter, we present the current status and the subjects of the evaluation system used for public research institutes performing R&D by demonstrating the practices of evaluation from the viewpoint of outcomes for individual research units in the National Institutes of Advanced Industrial Science and Technology (AIST).

Strategy Formulation in Public Research Institutes

We begin with an introduction to the management structure of this set of research institutes, and then we explain the tasks involved for each element in the structure.

Outline of AIST. By integrating the 15 individual institutes in the old AIST, the new AIST was reorganized as one of the R&D-performing Independent Administrative Institutions (IAI) linked to the Ministry of Economic, Trade, and Industry (METI) in 2001. The old institutes covered the research fields of biotechnology, electronic and information technology, mechanical technology, and energy and environmental technology, among others. The major features of the new AIST are (1) a huge institute including 2,500 core researchers; (2) diverse research fields of *interdisciplinary research* to realize long-range governmental policies focusing on the current and future needs of society, such as environment and energy; *advanced research* to explore broad spectra of research fields and integrate multidisciplinary subjects, such as life science and technology, information technology, nanotechnology, materials, and manufacturing; and *fundamental research* to develop and maintain high metrology standards for scientific and engineering research, such as geological surveying and applied geosciences; and (3) forming a flat organization composed of about 60 research units (research centers, research institutes, and research initiatives) to promote higher research flexibility and fluidity.

Research centers, committed to performing pioneer and strategic projects within 7 years are given priority in research resources and are operated by top-down management. Research institutes performing medium- range and long-term research select research subjects in a bottom-up manner. Research initiatives aim to be new research centers or research institutes within a short period (that is, less than 3 years).

Full Research. Traditional basic research is defined as Type-I Basic Research, which is mainly pursuit and discovery of novel laws, principles, and theories that govern natural phenomena. AIST defines Type-II Basic Research as research that integrates multiple disciplines and creates methods for use of integrated knowledge. AIST places its highest priority on pursuit of complete research ("Full Research"), which ranges from Type-I Basic Research to development of "products" by conducting intensive Type-II Basic Research. Contributions to industrial transformation are to be realized through the achievements of Full Research in AIST (see Figure 2.1).

Strategy Formation. The activities to form the research strategy are as follows. The overall strategy is composed of the basic mission with its required four submissions, plus the overall goals and policies to be satisfied. The basic mission of AIST is to contribute to a sustainable society by offering innovative technologies for industrial transformation.

The four submissions are (1) contributing to industrial competitiveness through Full Research, (2) playing the role of innovation hub in society, (3) implementing industrial policies in the regional economy, and (4) contributing to industrial technology policies.

The overall goals are composed of five outcomes: (1) high-quality life with good health and longevity; (2) intelligent, safe, and secure life supported by advanced information services; (3) high industrial competitiveness and reduction of environmental load realized by new materials, parts, and manufacturing technology; (4) wealthy and comfortable life by overcoming environmental and energy issues; and (5) advanced industrial

Figure 2.1. Full Research as a Concept of R&D in AIST

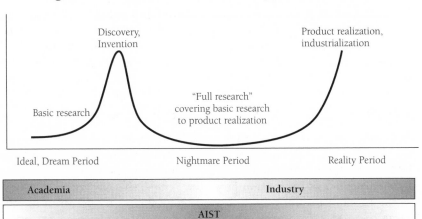

Figure 2.2. Strategy Structure of AIST for a Promising Future

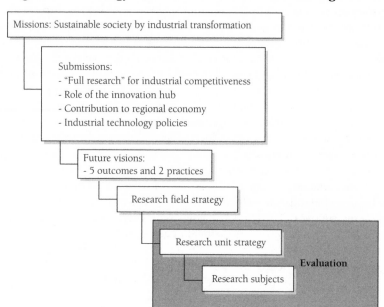

infrastructure developed by novel measurement technologies and evaluation systems. The two overall policies and practices required are (1) construction of an intellectual infrastructure through understanding of the earth and (2) dissemination of physical and chemical metrological standards (see Figure 2.2).

Strategy in each individual research field is composed of the strategic goal, the strategic research subjects, and focal research subjects. The strategic subjects are revised every year and gradually increase their content (technology portfolio, roadmaps, effective technology indices).

We expect the outcomes to be essential and substantial aspects of research achievements, such as recognition of research articles in a scientific society and valuable contents of socioeconomic products or services.

Research unit evaluation in AIST turns research unit strategy and research subjects into an object of evaluation.

Evaluation of R&D From the Perspective of Outcomes

AIST has strategically shifted the viewpoint from outputs to outcomes in the evaluation of research units at the beginning of the second research term (2005–2009) for effective and efficient execution of research.

Significance of Evaluation From the Perspective of Outcomes. AIST has the mission to innovate industrial technologies by performing Full Research in order to realize a sustainable society. It has been constructing the research strategies in the second research term on the basis of the mission. Each research unit is expected to produce socioeconomic values according to the mission and research strategy. Academic outcomes, such as prominent scientific papers, are also included in the socioeconomic values.

On the other hand, because it takes substantial time to realize such outcomes by applying the outputs, we decided to evaluate the process of R&D in each research unit from the viewpoint of outcomes. For this purpose, we have set three indices of evaluation: (1) *roadmap evaluation* to ask for a scenario of R&D aimed toward outcomes; (2) *output evaluation* to ask for potency for outcomes, namely research outputs with the possibility of contributing to the outcomes; and (3) *management evaluation* to ask for an outcome orientation in management of R&D in each research unit. In other words, our evaluation system is to reflect the future by anticipating the outcome to be realized. This style differs from the evaluation system in the first research term (2001–2004) on the basis of assessment of outputs (AIST, 2006a; Matsushita et al., 2004; Nakatsu et al., 2006).

Practical Evaluation From the Perspective of Outcomes

In this section, we discuss the significance of the new approach by looking at each component.

Roadmap Evaluation. We comprehensively evaluate the relevance of the research plan from the viewpoint of outcomes so as to put much emphasis on the appropriate research goals. We ask research units to develop clear roadmaps with outcomes as goals, milestones to the goal, and core technology elements in R&D, and we do benchmark comparison with other technologies or states of the relevant R&D in the world. We take into account the attributes of each kind of research unit (research center, research institute, or research initiative) and the characteristics of their research field (interdisciplinary researches, advanced research, or fundamental research) on evaluation.

Output Evaluation. We evaluate research outputs from the viewpoint of whether they are appropriate for producing eventual outcomes: papers, invited lectures, application for patent and registration of patents, creation of startups, prototype of new products, intellectual property, awards, and so on. We assess them on the basis of milestones and by comparing their level with the highest level in the world.

Management Evaluation. We evaluate the original approach to Full Research, efforts related to create innovation, efforts to cultivate human resources, and other activities, such as budget management and risk management.

Reviewers. The evaluation committee for each research unit was organized into external reviewers and internal reviewers. External reviewers, normally five to six members per individual evaluation committee for a research unit, are composed of specialists and intellectuals from academia, industry, and journalism. Internal reviewers are several principal reviewers who were nominated from the ranks of distinguished or experienced research leaders by the president of AIST. External reviewers give scores and comments in the roadmap evaluation and the output evaluation, and (only) comments for the management evaluation. Internal reviewers are mainly responsible for the management evaluation by way of giving scores and comments.

Scoring Method. Weighting of the score for the roadmap evaluation and the output evaluation by external reviewers relative to the weight of the score for management evaluation by internal reviewers was set to be seven to three. Points are awarded accordingly: AA = 5 (outstanding), A = 4 (good), B = 3 (adequate), C = 2 (inadequate), and D = 1 (poor).

Interval Between Evaluations. In the first research term (2001–2004), evaluation that had been performed every year was changed that so as to be every 2 years in the second research term (2005–2009). In 2005, research centers were the main recipients of an evaluation, whereas research institutes were the main recipients in 2006.

Inaugural Evaluation. Inaugural evaluations were performed when research institutes were beginning their second research term, or newly constructed research units were just starting their R&D activities, in order to supply reviews of roadmaps and management. They do not receive output evaluation in the inaugural evaluation.

Results of Evaluation From the Perspective of Outcomes

How well did this approach work? How well is it justified at this stage?

Roadmap Evaluation. The significance of setting clear outcomes has been well recognized by many of the research units. The roadmaps showing concrete outcomes, milestones, technology elements, and benchmarks have received high scores. On the other hand, many reviewers commented that more precise benchmarks would be desirable in a number of research units.

Output Evaluation. Reviewers gave high scores for outputs that showed excellence on the world-class ratings, significance, and impact of papers and patents, as well as in terms of originality, pioneering, and challenging "spirit of R&D."

Management Evaluation. Coherent and concurrent activity focused on Full Research, collaboration with enterprises for the innovation creation, efforts to get external human resources, nurturing of human resources inside and outside the research unit, communication between internal and external research units, strong leadership on the part of the unit director, acquisition of external funding, and efforts at risk management for accidents or inadequate achievements resulted in high scores on the evaluation of management.

External Reviews. According to the comments of reviewers, AIST has been recognized as having a clear common philosophy, managing research activities effectively and efficiently, and being a unique public institution to bridge basic research and applied research in Japan.

Reviewers also commented that the approaches to implementing Full Research in each research unit are admirable, but some of them needed to develop a tighter strategy with a clear scenario focusing on specific issues to be overcome.

Reviewers recognized that many research units showed good examples of roadmaps with clear outcomes as the ultimate goal, with the stages leading to that goal being based on the original high-potency technology. However, they also pointed that some roadmaps were not adequate because some of the milestones lacked concrete numbers, or had inadequate needs analysis, or used benchmarks without sufficient consideration of the global competitors, and so on. They also stated that roadmaps should be respecified according to progress in R&D and changes in the environmental context.

Moreover, some reviewers expressed concern that doing roadmap evaluation from the viewpoint of outcome may introduce some problems: (1) very basic research with high potential might not be done because of the difficulties in setting concrete outcomes, (2) R&D overall may be trivialized, and (3) completion of R&D will be limited according to how it is started.

Examples of the Research Unit Evaluation Reports

Here, we offer typical examples of the outcomes presented by the research units (AIST, 2006a). These reports have indeed disclosed the diverse features of the outcomes.

Correlated Electron Research Center (CERC). CERC aims at exploring new quantum-functional materials and developing new quantum devices on the basis of emerging physical science about "correlated electron systems." The term represents the state of matter where many electrons are strongly interacting with each other, forming liquid, solid, and liquid-crystal-like states. The outcomes from CERC are thought to be (1) creation of basic concepts and theory for the science of correlated electron systems, (2) development of a new research field of the science and technology of correlated electron systems, and (3) dissemination of new quantum devices that are based on correlated electron systems. The evaluation report has indicated that these outcomes are appropriate and the roadmaps, milestones, and concrete goals are set according to the clear vision of CERC. The quality of the outputs (scientific papers) is extremely high and the management of the research unit leader is suitable for the R&D of this field. Because this research center is going to be closed in 2008, future extension of this research field is one of the important topics in AIST.

Power Electronics Research Center (PERC). PERC aims at developing power semiconductors that can perform ultra-low-loss, high-speed, and high-temperature operation through research and development of wideband gap semiconductors such as SiC (silicon carbide) and GaN (gallium nitride). The concept of the total research solution comes from the basic research on materials and process technologies used in fabricating these semiconductor devices as power devices, possibly as far as development of prototype power converters, which are thought to be eventual research outcomes of PERC. Development of new design techniques for circuits, elemental parts, materials, packaging, and also reliability, along with system design for introducing excellent power device units into the nodes of electric power networks, are necessary and also thought to be important research outcomes. The evaluation report has concluded that the roadmaps, milestones, and outputs are suitable in order to achieve the mission; that creation of the startups for the SiC water supply is highly rated; and that future collaboration with industries is especially necessary.

The Research Center for Chemical Risk Management (CRM). CRM is engaged in research activities in chemical risk assessment and management that support maintaining a good balance between environmental safety and use of chemical substances. CRM's activities are founded on three pillars: basic research, practical research, and contributing to society. Society outreach to disseminate the outcomes of the research activities in risk assessment and management is one of the important missions of CRM. One of the typical outputs (and also outcomes) is publication of "risk assessment documents." The major features of CRM risk assessment documents are (1) application of new methods and techniques, (2) peer consultations with outside experts, and (3) socioeconomic evaluation of options for risk management. The evaluation committee rated highly the roadmaps and results for publication of the risk assessment documents for 30 chemical substances, as well as the challenging goals for new projects on multiple risk assessment.

Reaction of Staff to the Evaluation. We sent out questionnaires to each research unit to determine the utility of the evaluation system in AIST. According to the results of this survey, the evaluation has been accepted as useful in improving management of R&D, enough so as to compensate for the extra work it required.

Problems to Be Overcome. Many research units claimed that it was difficult to compose a suitable roadmap to relate their R&D strategy to outcomes. To design a suitable roadmap, a logic model could be useful, enabling us to connect the strategic scenario with defining resources and activities; appropriate outputs; the customers to receive outputs; and direct outcomes, intermediate outcomes, and indirect outcomes as ultimate goals (Jordan, Mortensen, Reed, & Teather, 2004).

Another issue for R&D evaluation is relating the evaluation for the research field to a higher level of strategy. This should be done in the next generation of evaluation systems in AIST. METI has published a Strategic Technology Roadmap, which consisted of (1) a scenario for dissemination,

(2) a technology overview, and (3) a technology roadmap. This roadmap covers many research fields, such as information and communications, life sciences, environment and energy, and manufacturing. It can be used as a reference for the R&D strategy, a tool for developing new R&D programs, and a method for allocating public R&D resources, as well as being a reference for evaluating ongoing programs (METI, 2007).

Reflections on the Evaluation

In this section, we reflect on our evaluations and also on a spiraling chain of R&D evaluation results.

Practical Payoffs From the Evaluation. R&D evaluation results including comments or advice from the reviewers should be put to practical use in R&D and its management. The major purposes of the research unit evaluation in AIST are to (1) encourage research unit activities, (2) give advice and suggestions to AIST top management, and (3) show accountability to various sectors of the nation. At the stage of constructing new research units, useful comments by reviewers of the evaluation committee are valuable in optimizing the environment necessary for R&D in terms of funds, researchers, space, facilities, and so on. The proposed goals should be reviewed in light of the specific comments.

Intermediate (formative) evaluation may indicate a different level of attainment at a set point, in contrast to the expected level. The research unit director should try to put these comments to practical use in the next stage, rather than maintaining the research using conventional facilities in a prearranged way.

Final (summative) evaluation summarizes all the activities of the research units, from strategy to research outputs and expected outcomes. The results of the final evaluation should be reflected in the products of new research units or development of the corresponding research field.

The PDCA (Plan-Do-Check-Action) cycle requires a practical process to improve the way of thinking and develop effective research. Evaluation results should be spirally fed back to the action part to construct renewal strategies.

In the case of AIST, the first impact of the evaluation results is with the research units. The director of a research unit should take the results for improvement of the research goals, resource allocation, and management in the unit. The next effect is in the research field in AIST. The direction of the corresponding field is thought over in view of the evaluation results. The final effect is for top management of AIST. Several judgments, such as resource allocation, R&D planning, and new R&D directions are made in this process.

A Spiral Chain of Strategic Evaluation. One of the main aims of strategic evaluation is steady practice of the PDCA process in the research

Figure 2.3. Spiral Chain of Reflection on R&D Evaluation Results

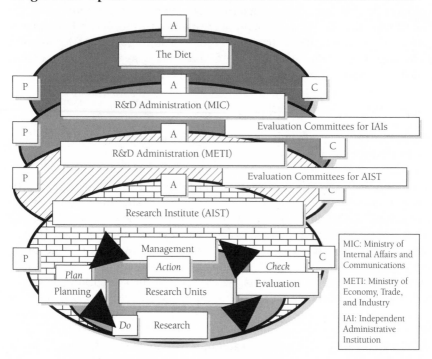

organization. More important, however, is that the spiral chain of PDCA cycles from the research unit level up to the Diet level should be effectively linked with each other (see Figure 2.3). It is also necessary to be consistently and optimally strategic; imperfect linkage of the PDCA chain system cannot yield the full benefits of strategic research evaluation in the nation.

The Future Vision

In this section, we discuss our vision for the future of assessing R&D outcomes, ideals for more effective evaluations of research, and the contribution of such evaluations to innovation.

Insight Into Outcomes. We have defined the outcome of the R&D in AIST to be the socioeconomic effects caused by outputs of R&D. This outcome has, in principle, many dimensions, among them dissemination of products, new theories, new research fields, new services, energy and natural resource savings, improved risk management, and disaster prevention. The time interval before realization of these outcomes of the R&D varies widely from immediately after the R&D project termination to a few decades after the project. For example, the risk management documents in the CRM are a short-term outcome, and dissemination of the new quantum devices on the correlated electron system in the CERC is a long-term outcome. Although some outcomes are easily evaluated as to where the benefits can be directly translated into monetized form, other outcomes are evaluated by noneconomic benefits to society (Georghiou & Roessner, 2000; Roessner, 2002). We should understand the expected outcomes of R&D as widely and deeply as possible, because the results of the research include many uncertain aspects owing to the intrinsic nature of the research.

Ideal Use of Intrinsic Research Evaluation. Research evaluation is expected to work effectively for people in many sectors, including the one where the R&D is promoted, the sector where investment in the research is achieved, and the sector where the benefits of the research are received. It is, however, essential not to spoil the intrinsic value of the research—that is, not let the evaluation "close down the future." It is also important that the evaluation encourage the researchers and the research institutes. On the other hand, it should be expected that the path to the most effective outcome will be highlighted through the research evaluation.

The intrinsic value of the research is essentially related to the fact that the research is an activity aimed to let us know what we don't know now, or to create what we don't have now. The value of the research is increased if the result of the research can contribute not only to expansion of humankind's knowledge, but also to the future of society and the earth. When we recognize that research is a creative action that produces what is not present now, it is clear that "essential evaluation" of research is, in principle, difficult.

Strategic Evaluation From the Perspective of Innovation. Innovation is defined as creation of novel social and economic values by science and technology. In September 2006, the Japanese Cabinet set up an Innovation 25 Strategy Council to study long-term strategy initiatives for creation of innovation until 2025.

Contributing to creation of innovation is one of the primary missions of the public research institutes for R&D. Given that, as mentioned earlier, it is difficult to forecast what specific outcomes can contribute to innovation, an effort to develop a suitable evaluation procedure to analyze the process from R&D to an effective outcome might be useful in tying R&D evaluation to the possibility of creating innovation.

Strategy and the scenario are crucial issues in the R&D activities in the public research institutes. Feedback of evaluation results to the next strategy is also important, which means that a mid- or long-term SDCS (Strategy-Do-Check-Strategy) cycle is necessary in addition to the short-term PDCA cycle in the R&D process for innovation.

Conclusions

We have described a novel evaluation system for the research units in AIST. The important issues are to (1) promote coherent and concurrent research, from basic research to development (Full Research) on the basis of a strategy for bringing about outcomes; (2) perform the evaluation from the viewpoint of outcomes, so as to have a clear scenario that can be related to future innovation; (3) influence evaluation results on the next strategy formation (SDCS); and (4) create spiral linkage of evaluation systems in various evaluation layers. This system can realize true strategic evaluation in the public research institute.

References

Evaluation Department, National Institute of Advanced Industrial Science and Technology (AIST). (2006a). *Report on research unit evaluation of AIST in FY2005* (in Japanese). Tsukuba, Japan: AIST.

Evaluation Department, National Institute of Advanced Industrial Science and Technology (AIST). (2006b). *Report on research unit evaluation of AIST in the first research term* (in Japanese). Tsukuba, Japan: AIST.

Georghiou, L., & Roessner, D. (2000). Evaluating technology programs: Tools and methods. *Research Policy, 29,* 657–678.

Jordan, G., Mortensen, J., Reed, J., & Teather, G. (2004, April). *Using logic model in managing performance of research and technology programs.* Paper presented at the meeting of International Association for Management of Technology, Washington, DC.

Matsushita, T., et al., (2004, October). *Research unit evaluation system of AIST.* Paper presented at the meeting of the Society of Project Management, Tokyo.

METI. (2007). *Strategic technology roadmap.* Retrieved September 9, 2007, from http://www.meti.go.jp/english/information/downloadfiles/PressRelease/070423STR2007.pdf.

Nakatsu, S., et al. (2006, November). *Introduction and reformation of an evaluation system in AIST.* Paper presented at the meeting of the American Evaluation Association, Portland, OR.

Roessner, D. (2002, February). *Outcome measurement in the United States: State of the art.* Paper presented at the meeting of American Association for the Advancement of Science, Boston.

OSAMU NAKAMURA is director of the industrial science and technology program management at AIST headquarters.

OSAMU NAKAMURA is counselor to the Evaluation Department in AIST.

MICHIKO TAKAGI SAWADA is a deputy director of the Evaluation Department in AIST.

SHIN KOSAKA is a deputy director of the Evaluation Department in AIST.

MASAO KOYANAGI is a principal reviewer of the Evaluation Department in AIST.

ISAO MATSUNAGA is a principal reviewer of the Evaluation Department in AIST.

KOICHI MIZUNO is a principal reviewer of the Evaluation Department in AIST.

NAOTO KOBAYASHI is a vice president of AIST.

Mallon, B. (2008). A peer review process for games and software. In C. L. S. Coryn & M. Scriven (Eds.), *Reforming the evaluation of research. New Directions for Evaluation, 118*, 37–45.

3

A Peer Review Process for Games and Software

Bride Mallon

Abstract

A peer-review process for assessing the contribution of artifacts, such as games and software to research, is proposed. Games and software produced as research output by academics tend to be accredited within their institution through discussion of the artifact, rather than directly. An independent judgment by peers confirming an artifact's contribution of something new, conceptually or practically, to a discipline can then be used by academics as evidence in secondary research appraisals, such as promotion appraisals or research assessment exercises, an example being the United Kingdom's Research Assessment Exercise. © Wiley Periodicals, Inc.

I n practice-based disciplines such as information systems or computer science, it seems ironic that assessment of the quality of research is so strongly weighted toward the academic paper, more than toward any other artifact or product-based research outcome. Frequently, academics do not get sufficient career credits from academic institutions for producing games, simulations, and software. As one academic complained at a recent conference, "I spent three years working on a simulation and three weeks on a paper, yet I got more credit from my institution for the paper than the

NEW DIRECTIONS FOR EVALUATION, no. 118, Summer 2008 © Wiley Periodicals, Inc.
Published online in Wiley InterScience (www.interscience.wiley.com) • DOI: 10.1002/ev.259

simulation." Consequently, academics tend to approach games and software simulations by producing written materials (such as design guidelines or evaluations or analysis of the development process) around the artifact, rather than to seek greater involvement in creation of the artifacts themselves; a large time commitment to creation is rarely possible and may indeed be detrimental to career prospects. However, limited involvement in artifact production can have a negative impact on the quality of reflection and research.

A key factor influencing this imbalance is that a well-established process for accrediting written materials, for judging their contribution and quality, exists—the peer review process—whereas a comparable process for judging and accrediting the artifacts themselves does not. This chapter argues for a peer review process for games and simulations and suggests how such a process might work operationally, and how an artifact may be judged and accredited by peer academics and industry developers.

Opposing the contention that such artifacts do not get sufficient academic credit, it might be argued that research assessment processes such as the United Kingdom's Research Assessment Exercise (RAE) do, in fact, contain some facilities to recognize artifacts, such as software or games. For example, the UoA (unit of assessment) 37 Library and Information Management Research Outputs subpanel (which includes disciplines concerned with management of information and knowledge in all formats, notably librarianship and information science, archives and records management, and information systems) "recognises that work may be submitted in [forms other than articles, books, chapters in books, and monographs, including research reports], and will not regard any type of output as being intrinsically of higher quality than another" (RAE 2008, 2007a, 2007b).

However, such inclusive guidelines may be discounted at the level of particular institutions, partly because of lack of a peer review. A key difficulty is that merely producing a new game or simulation or software should not be sufficient to gain research merits and credit. A key question that needs to be answered is, Does it actually constitute scientific research or advancement? To gain research "credits," an artifact should have instrumental scientific usage: Does it offer something new, conceptually or practically?

This key question—to what extent the artifact contributes to scientific advancement—must be answered, because this is the primary basis for evaluating research. As significant to artifact as to paper review is the question of the artifact's originality or contribution (bearing in mind the many types of originality). Is the contribution in the application area, or a new context of the simulation or game—for instance, an old role-play or adventure or strategy game applied to a new business training context? Does it answer some new problem or need? Does it solve a known problem more effectively or efficiently? Is the contribution a technical innovation? If the artifact is a computer simulation, perhaps its contribution might lie in modeling the real-world context it simulates more realistically than other products modeling that context? Is the contribution a new interaction strategy that will be adopted? Does an educational product go further in achieving higher learning goals within the particular topic it purports to teach than do similar products? (For example, using Bloom's hierarchy of educational objectives, does it go further than similar products in achieving learning goals to the end of the taxonomy of Knowledge, Comprehension, Application, Analysis, Synthesis, and Evaluation?). Or if the artifact implements a particular principle—say, a usability principle—does the artifact contribute to scientific advancement by testing, say, the utility of this principle in a particular context? Does the artifact test a particular theory? Does the artifact represent some increment or innovation or evolution that justifies its inclusion in the permanent record of the discipline?

Without specification of originality or contribution, some relevance or added value, there is inadequate justification for including the artifact in an academic peer review, which traditionally is premised on the notion that the work should advance science.

Here are conceivable benefits of a peer review process for software and games:

- Credit for these "publications" may be sought by academics, the artifact having been judged and evaluated by peers.
- Offering standards for games and software evaluation. Many software products, even highly expensive products, disappoint, do not fulfill their function, or fulfill it to a limited degree. A peer review process would help to overcome this problem by reducing opportunities for any weakness in the artifact to be disguised, presenting standards to achieve and rubberstamping the achievement of those standards.
- Furnishing accreditation of products for industry developers. Although this chapter argues for the importance of a peer review process to enable academics' artifacts to be judged as contributors to science, and industry developers have less need for such a process (given that the product can be successful without such contribution), a similar evaluation process for industry productions would also be valuable in highlighting and accrediting any originality or innovativeness in the artifacts.
- Giving formative feedback to authors or developers for improving products.
- Supplying publication outlets to serve as repositories for knowledge. Documentation and distribution of available games and simulations through the publication outlets will assist access for the individual or organization seeking to use them.

Before continuing, a note to clarify what I mean by peer review of "artifacts." I mean that the product will be reviewed during its performance, as it plays, as it is realized or materialized or performed. For example, a face-to-face game for teaching purposes will be sent to an instructor, a reviewer who tests the game with students. Software will be tried and tested: The reviewer will explore it, set up tasks within it, or try preset tasks. The artifact itself will be reviewed—as distinct from a paper about the artifact. Further, to clarify terminology, the term *artifact* is used in this chapter narrowly, referring to a traditional (face-to-face style) game, a computer game, a simulation, or a software product. In the wider usage of the term, artifacts could also refer to paper-based products. Nevertheless, to maintain the distinction that is central to this chapter's argument, the label *artifact* is reserved for products that are not, at least during their performance, paper-based.

Approaches for evaluating games and software are recommended in the next section. The section after that suggests how an artifact peer review process might be operationalized. The final section of this chapter discusses further research and remaining questions that need to be answered; it also reviews the benefits of such a process for various communities.

Evaluation Criteria

Evaluation of games and software is difficult and often controversial, but a particularly fruitful set of approaches in literature can be found in design and analytical science evaluation approaches. Following Klabbers (2006, 2007), I argue that recognition of analytical and design sciences distinctions is crucial because they directly affect the evaluation criteria appropriate for artifact assessment, and thus peer review. If the evaluator plans "to assess the impact of the game—the artifact—on its context-of-use with the purpose of improving the quality of ongoing affairs" (Klabbers, 2007, July), then the purpose is design science and the artifact should be assessed by design science evaluation criteria (such as usability). Conversely, developing and testing (game) theories belongs to the domain of the analytical sciences (Klabbers, 2007). If the evaluator intends to test a theory, analytical science evaluation criteria (such as validity and reliability) should be used. These design and analytical science classifications apply as much to software artifacts as to game artifacts.

These distinctions help to deconstruct artifacts by assessment purpose, pointing to the appropriate evaluation criteria and evaluation methodologies for each. They also warn assessors—not to mix up evaluation purposes. Klabbers (2007) stresses that a "quasi-analytical science" approach should not be applied to the (game) design sciences.

The goal of design science is to create artifacts, develop knowledge for design and realization of artifacts, solve construction problems (as architects and civil engineers do), or be used in improving the performance of existing entities (to solve improvement problems, as medical doctors and psychotherapists intend; Van Aken, 2004). This design science goal is compared alternatively in the literature to the natural sciences goal (to understand and explain the "real" world, as in biology or physics; Simon, 1996), the behavioral sciences goal (to develop and verify theories that explain or predict human and organizational behavior; Hevner, March, Park, & Ram, 2004), and the explanatory sciences (which describe, explain, and predict; Van Aken, 2004) as well as the analytical sciences. These goals are largely descriptive, whereas design science is prescriptive. Design science has its roots in the study of things created by humans, in the sciences of the artificial, and fundamentally it is concerned with human interventions to develop or improve an artifact.

Design science research incorporates research into an artifact's conceptual underpinnings—for instance, constructs, models, processes, and procedures that enable developers to understand and resolve the problems inherent in instantiating the material artifact—but these are addressed by the peer review process advocated in this chapter only through the instantiation, the material artifact (which embodies or generates or tests the more conceptual underpinnings).

The significance of the analytical and design science distinction for evaluation is now illustrated through a discussion of one key difference between them. Design scientists build their artifacts to function in well-defined contexts of use—in other words, for a specified problem domain (Hevner et al., 2004). Therefore, evaluators must examine not just the artifact but also the tie between the artifact and the environment within which it operates. Klabbers (2006) explains:

> The design style of enquiry does not produce general theoretical, or universal context-independent knowledge, which is the purpose of the analytical science. It is a science, an art and also a craft. Design scientists produce and apply knowledge for unique circumstances in order to create usable artifacts. Design science consists of constructing artifacts for special purposes and for assessing their impact under the well-defined circumstances of use. A basic question that needs to be addressed is: How well does the artifact perform, considering the specifications for the design, including the goals to be achieved? Contrary to the theory-driven approach of the analytical science, *the design science is issue driven*. It addresses human needs, conquers bottlenecks and capitalizes on opportunities. (p. 154)

This means that criteria addressing relevance (for a particular context) become more important in evaluating an artifact built for design science purposes (to change an existing situation into a preferred one) than in evaluating an artifact intended for analytical-science purposes (to generate or test a theory), because the former is not intended to be generally applicable, but to serve a particular purpose and need. It is important, therefore, to highlight that relevance for a particular context should have a stronger weighting in a design science artifact peer review than in an analytical science artifact peer review.

NEW DIRECTIONS FOR EVALUATION • DOI: 10.1002/ev

The issue of relevance for a particular context illustrates one key difference between the sciences, but other evaluation criteria, such as utility for solving previously unsolved problems (or known problems more effectively or efficiently) and usability, also become more predominant in design science assessment. Moreover, different methodologies and types of causal inferencing distinguish the design and analytical sciences. For example, with regard to the issue of causal inferencing, the causal model—which tries to explain "how the inputs and outputs are related, rather than simply noting the relationship" (Crowston, 2002, p. 151)—is more widely used in the design sciences. For a fuller discussion of the differences as they apply to games, see Klabbers (2006), and for a study of design science applied to a wider range of artifacts, see Hevner et al. (2004), March & Smith (2005), Simon (1996), and Van Aken (2004).

Operationalizing a Peer Review Process for Games and Simulations

There are a number of review models, such as journals publishing articles on editorial acceptance alone, and others sending articles blind to referees; another model makes the end articles freely available via the Internet, enabling readers to comment on archived articles, thus engaging the community-of-interest in the review process (although unless the interested community are peers, this is not peer review and does not serve a formative evaluation role). Another possibility is for established gaming and simulation and software organizations—rather than journals—to administer peer review of submitted artifacts.

Here are suggested procedures for operationalizing a peer review process for software and games.

Existing electronic journal publishers would supply online space for publication of the artifact, or a demonstration/exemplar of the artifact. A demonstration (demo) will replace full artifact publication if (1) software is too large for online publication, (2) software is not Web-enabled, or (3) authors and producers do not desire full online distribution. Copyright procedures for artifact publication may differ from paper publication. Currently, authors submitting papers assign copyright, or at least publication rights, to the publishers. However, if the game or software is commercially exploitable, authors may not wish to give copyright of the full artifact to the publisher or make the full artifact available over the Internet. In this case, assignment of copyright only to the publisher of the demonstration is more feasible.

The online demonstration may be a working demo or graphics accompanied by textual description. In such cases, the journal will supply facilities to distribute the full game description or full software to reviewers by alternative means (such as mailing a DVD). Reviewers must be qualified to review such artifacts; ideally, they will be people with experience in using similar artifacts in the same content area (if natural language processing software is to be reviewed, reviewers should already be familiar with a range of natural language processing software) and people with expertise in the content area (if a face-to-face game to teach Porter's value chain is to be reviewed, the reviewer will be an information or business systems instructor). Using a number of reviewers will strengthen the process.

The artifact will be accompanied by written documentation prepared by its authors/developers, which contains:

- Categorization of the game or software, similar to many such categorizations supplied by journals, for instance, the ACM system: subject content: language processing > natural language processing > kind: software > subject content: business > management training > leadership training > kind: face-to-face game.
- Specification of the claimed research contribution. This will be accompanied by a review of antecedent or comparable product features and literature on such products (to supply evidence that the claimed contribution is indeed a contribution). It will help to frame the contribution in comparison to, or as an extension of, prior developments.
- An answer to whether the artifact satisfies any additional criteria supplied by the particular journal. (In the same way that journals have differing foci, artifact publishers will have their own foci and specialties—management training, financial modeling, language learning, language translation, supply-chain management, change management, and cultural studies.)

On completion of the review process, the journal outlet will publish the artifact in full or as a demonstration. The artifact or demonstration will be accompanied by the written documentation (modified in accordance with the reviewers' critiques). This will include anonymous reviewers' stamp of approval of any claimed contribution—a specification of whether the claimed contribution is true, in their opinion.

There are a number of advantages of building artifact review on the back of existing paper journal outlets. Some administrative processes, such as editorial structures, networking with reviewers, establishing assessment criteria for reviewers, established foci (for instance, language learning, management training, stock market modeling, and so on), and Internet sites (adaptable for hosting, distributing, and archiving the artifact, in full or demonstration form), are already in place. Academics working in an area are likely already to be familiar with the journals, reducing marketing requirements; therefore, acceptance of artifacts as "publications" within academic circles (the goal driving this chapter) may be eased by use of similar journal outlets and, moreover, may benefit from any status already attached to the particular journal.

Discussion and Conclusions

Future work requires further development of what constitutes an artifact's research contribution. Our suggestions so far (proffered in the introduction) pivot on whether the artifact offers new relevance: Can it be applied specifically and directly to solve a problem in a new or better way (instrumental relevance) or be used for general enlightenment (conceptual relevance) by throwing a new light on an issue, influencing actions but more indirectly and less specifically than in instrumental use? But there may be other dimensions along which a contribution can be defined. Even if the research contribution continues to pivot on the issue of relevance, relevance is multifaceted. Moreover, artifacts are used for widely differing purposes, have myriad features, and are diverse in terms of the contribution or innovation or evolution. Further work needs to be undertaken on explicating what an artifact's research contribution can be, when, why, and to whom, to assist judgment about its value for research or scientific advancement.

What kind of evidence will be needed to verify whether the claimed contribution is a contribution? The documentation accompanying the artifact giving the authors' review of antecedent or comparable product features or literature about such features will offer some evidence. Authors and artifact producers should review products in the area before making a contribution claim, and these findings will be used to answer questions on their own contribution claim and its predicted impact. A criterion for acceptance of the artifact for publication will be the comprehensiveness of the authors' attempt at framing their claimed contribution in comparison to, or as an extension of, prior innovations. Further evidence (and trust in the process) will come from careful selection of reviewers with expertise in the niche pertaining to the contribution.

One question motivating this special issue is, "How does the evaluation of research need reform?" This chapter criticizes current academic policy in some practice-based disciples such as information systems, where research assessment is so strongly weighted toward the paper that the artifact (vital to the practice-based discipline) is evaluated mainly through a secondary product: a paper about the artifact. How a peer review process might address artifact review is suggested here, and benefits are discussed primarily from the perspective of the individual academic. However, it should have benefits to many people: scientists, administrators, evaluators, and the public. Academics who produce games and software, who currently find their products undervalued in their institution, or worse are encouraged by current research policies not to devote their limited time to artifact production, would benefit from a process that rewards creation rather than smothering it. Institutions would have the results of an independent primary peer review process for judging artifact quality that will answer questions policy makers and funders of research need answered, such as what the research contribution and quality of an artifact are, and that may be used for secondary

NEW DIRECTIONS FOR EVALUATION • DOI: 10.1002/ev

peer review exercises (such as the UK's RAE). An understanding of criteria appropriate for artifact assessment (and differences and similarities between such criteria and paper-assessment criteria) will be refined through an artifact peer review process. Moreover, the process of operationalizing peer review according to design or analytical science distinctions should produce better evaluation tools for both. Finally, independent judgments of an artifact supplied as an output of peer review will help a member of the public in choosing an artifact.

This chapter suggests where and how games and software can be judged and how an artifact peer review process might be operationalized. Actually awarding career credits for games and software creation still depends on institutions or assessment bodies—this is separate from the peer review process—but their task would be facilitated by a peer review mechanism for judging the quality, value, and original contribution of the work.

References

Crowston, K. (2002). Process as theory in information systems research. *Proceedings of the IFIP WG 8.2 International Conference: The Social and Organizational Perspective on Research and Practice in Information Technology*. Retrieved April 25, 2005, from http://is.lse.ac.uk/Support/ifip_wg82/Aalborg/crowston.pdf

Hevner, A. R., March, S. T., Park, J., & Ram, S. (2004). Design science in information systems research. *MIS Quarterly, 28*(1), 75–105.

Klabbers, J. H. G. (2006). *The magic circle: Principles of gaming & simulation*. Rotterdam: Sense.

Klabbers, J. H. G. (2007, July). *Assessment methodology: The validity of my Ferrari*. Paper presented at the International Simulation and Gaming Association conference, Nijmegen, Netherlands.

March, S. T., & Smith, G. F. (2005). Design and natural science research on information technology. *Decision Support Systems, 15,* 251–266.

RAE 2008. (2007a). *UOA 37 library and information management*. Retrieved December 15, 2006, from http://www.rae.ac.uk./panels/main/i/library/

RAE 2008. (2007b). *UOA 37, Library and Information Management panel statement*. Retrieved December 2006, from http://www.rae.ac.uk/pubs/2006/01/docs/i37.pdf

Simon, H. A. (1996). *Sciences of the artificial* (3rd ed.). Cambridge, MA: MIT Press.

Van Aken, J. E. (2004). Management research based on the paradigm of the design sciences: The quest for field-tested and grounded technological rules. *Journal of Management Studies, 41*(2), 219–246.

BRIDE MALLON *is a lecturer in information systems at the School of Management and Economics, Queen's University Belfast, Northern Ireland. Her research interests include new-media narrative forms, gaming, and business simulation software.*

Donovan, C. (2008). The Australian Research Quality Framework: A live experiment in capturing the social, economic, environmental, and cultural returns of publicly funded research. In C. L. S. Coryn & M. Scriven (Eds.), *Reforming the evaluation of research. New Directions for Evaluation, 118,* 47–60.

4

The Australian Research Quality Framework: A Live Experiment in Capturing the Social, Economic, Environmental, and Cultural Returns of Publicly Funded Research

Claire Donovan

Abstract

The author regards development of Australia's ill-fated Research Quality Framework (RQF) as a "live experiment" in determining the most appropriate approach to evaluating the extra-academic returns, or "impact," of a nation's publicly funded research. The RQF was at the forefront of an international movement toward richer qualitative, contextual approaches that aimed to gauge the wider economic, social, environmental, and cultural benefits of research. Its construction and implementation sent mixed messages and created confusion about what impact is, and how it is best measured, to the extent that this bold live experiment did not come to fruition. © Wiley Periodicals, Inc.

Note: During 2006, the author was chair of the Department of Education, Science, and Training's (DEST) Research Quality Framework Development Advisory Group (RQFDAG) Technical Working Group on Research Impact. The views expressed in this chapter do not necessarily reflect those of the Working Group, the Development Advisory Group, or DEST.

NEW DIRECTIONS FOR EVALUATION, no. 118, Summer 2008 © Wiley Periodicals, Inc.
Published online in Wiley InterScience (www.interscience.wiley.com) • DOI: 10.1002/ev.260

47

Research funding organizations and science policy circles use the term *research quality* to describe the measurable influence of academic research on the academic community. Research impact denotes the benefits or returns from research, which flow beyond the academic realm to "end users" of research. These end users are traditionally defined as industry, business, government, or more broadly, the taxpayer. As I explain elsewhere (Donovan, 2007b), indicators of research quality such as research income and citation measures have become part of the fabric of research evaluation; in recent years, there has been growing interest in similarly evaluating research impact. This has been spurred by the desire on the part of governments to gauge the value of publicly funded research to end users beyond academia. The reasons for accounting for impact vary: to justify expenditure on academic research in terms of its return on taxpayers' investment, or to create public value for society; to redirect national science foresight planning toward relevant research; to enhance international industrial and economic competitiveness; and (in tandem with quality assessment) to inform performance-based distribution of block funding to universities.

Evolution of Research Impact Evaluation

The following distinct phases in the evolution of impact evaluation have been noted (Donovan, 2007b; Martin, 2007).

Technometrics. The initial search for reliable quantitative measures sought to collate data on investment from industry, commercialization, and technology transfer. However, these data were found to represent a low-order level of impact that did not extend to broader economic or societal benefits, and marked an unsophisticated approach to impact measurement confined to science, technology, engineering and medicine, and the concerns of industry and business (Donovan, 2006).

Sociometrics. A second phase of impact evaluation sought more socially relevant measures in the form of sociometrics, which attempted to map research outcomes onto existing government social statistics (Allen Consulting Group, 2005). Yet, these impact indicators presented no credible link between academic research and macro-level social trends, and they overlooked the cultural import of research.

Case Studies. A third wave of impact evaluations acknowledged that quantification may conceal more than it reveals. Typically employed by dedicated research funding organizations to assess the outcomes of specific funding initiatives, these evaluations proceeded on a case-study basis and sought to combine quality and impact measurements using both quantitative and qualitative (or deliberative) approaches. The case-studies generally attempted to gauge a more broadly conceived notion of impact, which probed various dimensions of the economic, social, and environmental returns from research. This approach demonstrates sensitivity to the definition of *impact*, which varies with the perspectives of such end users as government, citizens, consumers, business, industry, community groups, NGOs, and practitioners. These different perceptions affect what is valued and hence measured, and so case-study methodology includes several impact dimensions, and it encourages end-user participation throughout the evaluation process (Spaapen, Dijstelbloem, & Wamelink, 2007; Wooding, Hanney, Buxton, & Grant, 2004). Yet, this sophisticated case-study approach has been largely confined to evaluating the impact of scientific and medical research, and it has not been adapted to assessment of a nation's whole research base.

The International Context. In terms of national research assessment exercises, to date the most developed examples of impact evaluation have occurred in the Netherlands and New Zealand. These evaluations sit alongside quality assessment and primarily focus on the economic value of publicly funded research, while measures of broader user engagement are bound to low-level input and output indicators, rather than tangible societal benefits. Even so, the Netherlands seeks data on the influence of research on developments or questions in society at large, and New Zealand collects brief contextual descriptions of linkages beyond academia.

These innovations resonate with current concerns in the international research evaluation community, which has come to recognize the limited value of impact assessment tied exclusively to economic and quantitative concerns; the latest movement in impact evaluation is toward developing richer qualitative and contextual approaches at the national level (Donovan, 2007a; FWF/ESF, 2007). In this vein, the 2008 Australian Research Quality Framework (RQF) was the first national research assessment exercise to include a truly comprehensive and methodologically diverse impact audit.

A Brief History of RQF Development

Australia's RQF came into being as a hybrid solution to academic concerns about research quality and government interest in research impact. The Australian academic community wanted the government to allocate university block funding on the basis of discipline-based peer review of research quality rather than the extant metrics-based formula (DEST, 2004b). The government wanted to boost Australia's innovation strategy through linking academic research to the concerns of industry and business, particularly in the context of broader economic, social, and environmental benefits to society (DEST, 2004a). The RQF was proposed as a panel-based exercise to evaluate both research excellence and the wider benefits of academic research for the nation, and to allocate funds on the basis of outcomes. It is unsurprising, given the impact push from government and the quality pull from academia, that the RQF philosophy of impact evaluation was contested and reshaped throughout its development and implementation.

There were several phases of RQF development involving various advisory groups, technical working groups, and much consultation with the Australian higher education sector. In December 2004, the Minister for

Science, Education, and Training appointed an Expert Advisory Group (EAG), which launched a consultative exercise to determine the structure and features of the RQF (DEST, 2005c). The EAG published its preferred RQF model in September 2005 (DEST, 2005d) and gave its final advice in December 2005 (DEST, 2005b).

A new minister took office, and in March 2006, a new Development Advisory Group (DAG) was created, chaired by Australia's Chief Scientist and tasked to refine the RQF model and detail its phases of implementation. In June 2006, the Minister announced that the first RQF would take place in 2008, and the DAG appointed several technical working groups to address in detail various RQF features in need of further development. This included a Technical Working Group on Research Impact, which reported its findings to the DAG during August 2006.

The Technical Working Group on Research Impact. The Impact Working Group comprised senior academics, senior university managers, representatives from business and industry, experts in impact evaluation, and several DAG members. The membership also represented academic interests in science, technology, engineering, medicine, commerce, humanities, creative and performing arts, and social science. Its remit was to offer detailed advice to the DAG in these areas:

* Methodology: recommend the optimal methodology to assess the impact of Australia's universities
* Indicators: develop generic and discipline-specific quantitative and qualitative measures of research impact
* Assessment period: establish the appropriate length of the assessment period required for effectively assessing research impact
* Evidence portfolios: determine the necessary evidence for research groups to demonstrate impact, including composition of impact statements, metrics to be presented in context statements, and a decision whether "four best outputs per researcher" are adequate to demonstrate research quality and impact
* Demonstrating impact: advise how research groups are to demonstrate research impact, and how ratings of research impact are most effectively reported
* Verifying impact: propose appropriate processes for assessment panels to evaluate research impact

Various RQF features were fixed, and the Impact Working Group had to navigate around them. For example, the EAG had defined research impact as the "social, cultural, economic, and/or environmental outcomes for industry, government and/or other identified communities regionally within Australia, nationally and/or internationally" (DEST, 2005b, p. 24). Another key characteristic was the RQF being a panel-based peer and end-user review of the quality and impact of Australian university research. There were 13 panels, which were clusters of disciplines that shared similar assessment profiles (for example, physical, chemical and earth sciences; engineering and technology; social science and politics; law, education and professional practices; humanities, creative arts, design and built environment). The assessment will be conducted at the research-group level, rather than at the individual level (as in the case of the New Zealand Performance Based Research Fund) or the discipline level (like the United Kingdom Research Assessment Exercise). The quality assessment consisted of panel judgments combining a peer review of the four "best" outputs per researcher with quality metrics applied to research groups. In terms of impact assessment, set features were an impact scale against which to report and judge the level of research impact; and research groups submitting an impact statement linking the group's research to claimed impact outcomes, the beneficiaries, the measurable difference made by the research, and the details of end users who may confirm research groups' impact claims (DEST, 2005b).

Key Recommendations. The Impact Working Group met four times between June and August 2006. During this period, the DAG offered feedback through its members within the group and by way of DEST, sometimes suggesting that advice be modified—a demonstration of the government pull and academic push in action. At the request of the DAG, the Impact Working Group produced a short outline of its advice, highlighting changes or refinements to EAG recommendations. This was made public as a DAG "Guiding Principles" document in August 2006 (DEST, 2006d). The Impact Working Group presented its final report to the DAG in August 2006 (TWGRI, 2006); the DAG published a revised version of this advice in September 2006 (DEST, 2006b) and its final recommended RQF model in October 2006 (DEST, 2006c). The Impact Working Group's recommendations are summarized below, along with noteworthy deviations from EAG and DAG thinking.

Methodology. The optimum assessment methodology was a qualitative and contextual approach, mediated through the judgment of academic peers and end users. Information is best derived from context statements, impact statements, case studies, and (where appropriate) relevant quantitative and qualitative indicators (TWGRI, 2006).

Indicators. Quantitative metrics are underdeveloped and cannot be used as a proxy for determining impact ratings for research groups; but where appropriate, some qualitative and quantitative indicators may support impact claims (TWGRI, 2006). The DAG decided that assessment panels would nonetheless be given generic impact indicators and be asked to determine additional cluster-specific ones (DEST, 2006c).

Assessment Period. The EAG chose a 6-year assessment window (2001 to 2006) for quality and impact assessment and decided that the impact to be assessed must be related to research conducted within the same 6-year period. The Impact Working Group proposed that although the research impact assessed should occur within the 6-year window, it may be derived from original research conducted earlier (TWGRI, 2006), and assessment panels may use their judgment to determine a reasonable time frame from the original research to the impact claimed. These recommendations were endorsed by the DAG (DEST, 2006c). The Working Group believed cases where the original research is older than 15 years will require additional supporting evidence (TWGRI, 2006). The DAG limited the period for older research to an additional 6 years only (DEST, 2006c).

Evidence Portfolios. The following recommendations were made in terms of material to be included in evidence portfolios to best enable research groups to demonstrate impact:

1. Impact statements should be the basis of assessing research impact. They should be evidence-based, no more then 10 pages in length, and consist of a statement of claims against impact criteria, up to four case studies illustrating examples of impact, and details of end users who can verify the impact claims (DEST, 2006d).
2. No metrics are to be given in the context statement, but they may be used to support claims made in a research group's impact statement.
3. The EAG proposed the same four best outputs per researcher be used to assess both quality and impact claims. The Impact Working Group recommended that impact assessment should draw on a group's complete body of work, including nontraditional outputs such as reports to government (TWGRI, 2006), which amounted to a revision of the RQF model, a recommendation supported by the DAG (DEST, 2006b).

Demonstrating Impact. The following recommendations were given regarding evidence necessary to demonstrate research impact and how ratings of research impact are most effectively reported:

1. Research impact is best demonstrated by linking a group's impact claims to criteria set out in the impact rating scale. Evidence should connect the group's original research to impact ratings (TWGRI, 2006). The Impact Working Group recommended clear guidelines be developed at the discipline level, a proposal endorsed by the DAG (DEST 2006c).
2. Connecting impact claims to the impact rating scale is the most effective way to report claims of research impact. The EAG recommended a simple three-point scale demonstrating the degree of public benefit derived from research (DEST, 2005b). The Impact Working Group shared this preference, but the DAG directed it to develop a five-point scale with more attention to engagement with end users. The Impact Working Group's final scale was a blend of end-user interaction and public benefit, initially endorsed by the DAG (DEST, 2006d) but later modified by the DAG to reflect more commercial and industrial concerns (DEST, 2006b).

Verifying Impact. Assessment panels will review research groups' evidence portfolios and apply their collective expert judgment to determine the validity of the claims made against the impact criteria. Impact ratings will be assigned, and the rating process will be moderated between discipline panels to ensure consistency and fair treatment for multidisciplinary research. The Working Group recommended the Payback consensus scoring model as particularly suited for this purpose (TWGRI, 2006; Wooding, Hanney, Buxton, & Grant, 2004).

Contested Themes in the RQF Philosophy of Impact Evaluation

According to the Hon. Julie Bishop, Minister for Education, Science, and Training:

> It is my view that if we are able to get right the measure of impact—in both its form and its recognition—then we will have created a research evaluation measure that will greatly surpass those of other nations. (DEST, 2006a)

The role of impact evaluation in the RQF came with high expectations from government. As the minister elaborated, "It will ensure that not only do we, as a country, reward high quality research, but also we reward research which makes a demonstrable change to the way we live or enjoy our lives" (DEST, 2006d). However, the RQF philosophy of impact assessment has, at times, resembled the "pushmi-pullyu" of Dr. Dolittle fame: a two-headed llama that tries to travel in opposite directions. The government push toward impact is offset by a pull toward more scholarly concerns; this push is sometimes forcefully directed toward the interests of industry and commerce, yet counterbalanced by an equally strong pull toward broader public benefits (Donovan 2007c). It is within this context that the chapter now turns to examining central concepts in impact evaluation that display these inherent tensions: defining research impact, communicating research beyond academia, and accounting for research impact.

Defining Research Impact. For RQF purposes, impact was originally concerned with social, economic, and environmental effects, reflecting a trend toward "triple bottom line" accounting (Donovan, 2007b). The EAG's consultation with the higher education sector led to introducing the "cultural" as a fourth impact domain; and the resulting quadruple bottom line was unique in international impact assessment terms. When we turn to consider what, precisely, impact denotes, there are contradictory messages contained in the RQF deliberations, which reflect a fragile balance of push-pull interests.

The Impact Working Group alone supplied actual content for the four impact domains (DEST, 2006b; TWGRI, 2006), which was dropped by the DAG, but reintroduced in the 2007 submission specifications. Impact is described as adding to the social, economic, natural, and cultural capital of the nation:

- *Social Benefit.* "Improving quality of life; stimulating new approaches to social issues; changes in community attitudes, and influence upon developments or questions in society at large; informed public debate and improved policy-making; enhancing the knowledge and understanding of the nation; improved equity; and improvements in health, safety and security."
- *Economic Benefit.* "Improved productivity; adding to economic growth and wealth creation; enhancing the skills base; increased employment; reduced costs; increased innovation capability and global competitiveness; improvements in service delivery; and unquantified economic returns resulting from social and public policy adjustments."
- *Environmental Benefit.* "Improvements in environment and lifestyle; reduced waste and pollution; improved management of natural resources; reduced consumption of fossil fuels; uptake of recycling techniques; reduced environmental risk; preservation initiatives; conservation of biodiversity; enhancement of ecosystem services; improved plant and animal varieties; and adaptation to climate change."
- *Cultural Benefit.* "Supporting greater understanding of where we have come from, and who and what we are as a nation and society; understanding how we relate to other societies and cultures; stimulating creativity within the community; contributing to cultural preservation and enrichment; and bringing new ideas and new modes of experience to the nation."

We find that the Impact Working Group and early DAG documents define impact in terms of public benefit within these domains (DEST, 2006b, 2006d; TWGRI, 2006). On the other hand, the EAG and the DAG's recommended RQF are concerned with direct practical utility and more targeted groups of end users; for example, *impact* is interchanged with the word *usefulness* (DEST, 2005a) and is "the recognition by qualified end-users that quality research has been successfully applied to achieve social, cultural, economic, and/or environmental outcomes" (DEST, 2005b, p. 12; DEST, 2006c, p. 10); it is found in "short-term . . . outcomes for industry, government and/or other identified communities" (DEST, 2005a, p. 24). We shall see that when considering impact domains and impact rating scales, these divergent views entail mixed messages about what constitutes legitimate impact and how it may be measured and verified.

Finally, when looking at how impact is defined, it is important to note what is excluded. First, the RQF immediately rejected the notion of impact as "knowledge transfer," for example, commercialization of other people's ideas (DEST, 2005d). In this respect, impact may be purely related to a research group's own original research. Second, a research group may apply for exclusion from impact assessment if its research is at an early stage of development, or if its research orientation means it would be inappropriate to be assessed in terms of impact (DEST, 2005b, 2006b, 2006c). Third, contrary to European developments (FWF/ESF, 2007), basic research is exempted from impact assessment on the grounds that it is not devalued (DEST 2005b, 2006b; TWGRI, 2006): ". . . The fundamental research of today may yield the research impact of the future. In this respect, impact assessment must allow for progress from initial research through to eventual impact, and acknowledge that this is not a necessarily linear process, and that this development takes time" (TWGRI, 2006, p. 2).

However, the "pull" of this sentiment is at odds with the DAG's decision to allow only an additional 6-year window to connect original research to impact; it is a counterintuitive short-term push that devalues basic research through excluding many significant and enduring research impacts from evaluation.

Communicating Research Beyond Academia. During RQF development, there were differing views on what form of publication should be used to link a group's original research to its impact claims. The EAG had recommended that the same best four outputs per researcher be used for both quality and impact assessment (DEST, 2005b). However, this failed to recognize that vehicles for communication differ for academic and nonacademic audiences. It also led to concerns that a linear ideal of scientific discovery underpinned the impact assessment model—that a group of scientists publish a journal article, the idea is taken up and developed, and impact for society is then accrued in terms of technical or health benefits, for example. The Impact Working Group argued that "the types of research output one would submit to demonstrate quality and impact are often quite different because these publications are tailored for different audiences." It recommended that nontraditional outputs, such as reports for government, public exhibitions, and media broadcasts, were an essential link between original research and engagement with end users, and so should be separately drawn on for impact assessment. It also argued that impact occurring within the 6-year assessment period is likely to be connected to traditional and nontraditional research outputs produced before the 6-year window for quality assessment, and thus the window for impact should be extended (TWGRI, 2006). The DAG endorsed these sentiments (DEST, 2006b, 2006c).

In this instance, the push was led by the Impact Working Group's search for the optimum methodology for impact assessment, which polarized the Australian university sector because this preference was supported by technical universities and opposed by the pull of elite academic institutions for an RQF giving primacy to peer review of "high-quality" publications.

Accounting for Research Impact. As has been noted, divergent views of what impact is entail differing views of what should be measured and how. The "push" toward impact as industrial and commercial advance finds its ultimate expression in quantitative metrics tied to investment from business and industry, patents, and commercialization; the pull toward public value seeks to make previously intangible public benefits of research visible by employing a contextual approach, informed by qualitative and quantitative evidence, and judged by academic peers and end users. Drawing on international best practice in impact evaluation, and strongly favoring a case study approach to methodology, the Impact Working Group supported the latter position. However, we can easily imagine both approaches adopting a panel system informed by evidence supporting a scale of impact claims against the four impact domains presented in the section Defining Research Impact earlier, albeit in a largely quantitative or more contextual manner (potential examples are presented in TWGRI, 2006). Hence, the principle of the case study approach was endorsed by the DAG, as indeed was the continued search (in vain) for more valid metrics of high-order impact (DEST, 2006a).

The impact scale was perhaps the most hotly contested aspect of RQF impact evaluation. As has been noted, during RQF deliberations, the impact scale morphed from a simple three-point measure of degrees of wider benefit, to a fine-grained five-point scale geared to end-user interaction. The actual RQF scale is presented in the next section and matches the DAG preference (DEST, 2006a). It is a linear, progressive scale, premised on a route to impact that begins with (1) engagement with end users who recognize the importance of the research to a defined area, (2) adoption of research, (3) adoption producing benefits for end users, and (4) and (5)evidence of the magnitude of the benefit derived from the adoption. On the other hand, the Impact Working Group's alternative scale was nonlinear, preferring (1) reciprocal engagement with end users, (2) significant uptake of research by the end-user community, (3) significant added value or improvements, and entailing (4 and 5) transformational benefits on a large scale. It was felt that although the language of "adoption" was suited to an idealized model of practice in engineering with industry as the end user, it alienated the humanities, arts, and social sciences. The "pull" was toward a more inclusive scale, which would embrace all disciplines, and the diffuse manner in which research has value beyond academia; the "push" was concerned with targeted end-user engagement and driving behaviors that would make Australia's science base more efficient.

Australia's Live Experiment

RQF development continued throughout 2007, including a series of discipline workshops that each devoted half a day to research impact; further sector consultations; RQF trials, including testing mechanisms for assessing research impact; and development of generic specifications and panel-specific guidance, which were released in September 2007 (DEST, 2007).

New Directions for Evaluation • DOI: 10.1002/ev

The generic specifications display a great deal of pull in that a repeated catchphrase is the usefulness of research for "government, industry, business and the wider community." The definition of impact is extended: "Impact refers to the extent to which research has led successfully to social, economic, environmental, and/or cultural benefits for the wider community, *or an element of the community*" (DEST, 2007, p. 5, emphasis added), which allows inclusion of private value in addition to public value. In terms of defining research impact, there is an explicit request that research groups should include in their impact statements "identifiable and supportable impact-related indicators. This requires the impact statement to identify the beneficiaries of the research and the way in which they have benefited" (DEST, 2007, p. 30). The "push" also dominates in the flavor of examples of impact given: "improved quality of products/services, cost-effectiveness, customer satisfaction, lives saved or productivity" (DEST, 2007, p. 33); "policy impacts can also include changes to policies of corporations, councils, professional groups and non-government organizations" (DEST, 2007, p. 33). A series of examples restricted to industry and psychology are given to illustrate outcomes that would match impact ratings from D to A (see Table 4.1).

The panel-specific guidance, however, does give tailored examples of engagement, uptake of research, and extent of benefit. Yet, no examples of impact metrics are offered. In this sense, the RQF remains a pushmi-pullyu, with the push at the grand policy level and the pull at the research group and panel level, leaving scope for contextual interpretation of the impact scale in discipline-specific terms.

Despite publication of the generic specifications and panel-specific guidance, we find that impact measurement in the RQF remained a live experiment as (1) its fine detail was left to be refined at the panel level,

Table 4.1. The Impact Rating Scale

Rating	Description
A	Adoption of the research has produced an outstanding social, economic, environmental, or cultural benefit for the wider community, regionally within Australia, nationally, or internationally.
B	Adoption of the research has produced a significant social, economic, environmental, or cultural benefit for the wider community, regionally within Australia, nationally, or internationally.
C	Research has been adopted to produce new policies, products, attitudes, behaviors, or outlooks in the end-user community.
D	Research has engaged with the end-user community to address a social, economic, environmental, or cultural issue, regionally within Australia, nationally, or internationally.
E	Research has had limited or no identifiable social, economic, environmental, or cultural outcome, regionally within Australia, nationally, or internationally.

although this lack of transparency was of vital concern for research groups in need of guidance to effectively construct their impact statements; and (2) the balance of quantitative indicators versus contextual evidence to inform the second RQF remained under review. The RQF was also a live experiment because of uncertainty over its future; there is a general election due in Australia, and the Labor Party, which was ahead in the polls the day the RQF specifications were released, has vowed that if it replaced the current Liberal coalition government, it would abandon impact assessment. There were suggestions that the RQF would take place in 2009 rather than 2008, and that impact measurement should be a shadow exercise in the RQF's first iteration.

The RQF approach to impact evaluation was a world first; other countries have tended to focus on economic returns or rely on quantitative rather than contextual approaches to impact assessment. The consequence has been that impact measurements prove unsatisfactory, largely because the public value of research has not been adequately addressed. The RQF certainly went a long way toward developing an optimal methodology for capturing the social, economic, environmental, and cultural returns of publicly funded research.

The pushmi-pullyu aspect of implementing a pluralistic impact evaluation may be part of an inevitable compromise of government and academic interests. However, this runs the danger of presenting mixed messages about what precisely research impact is and how best to account for it within a national research assessment exercise. This live experiment did not come to fruition.

Postscript

The Australian Labor Party won the 2007 general election, and on December 21, 2007, announced that the RQF would not proceed. Senator Kim Carr, the Minister for Innovation, Industry, Science and Research, argued that "The RQF is poorly designed, administratively expensive and relies on an 'impact' measure that is unverifiable and ill-defined" (IISR, 2007), The new Government is pursing an alternative evaluation system, Excellence for Research in Australia (ERA). Indications are that this will constitute a "quality" audit without "impact" assessment. In the meantime, impact evaluation is in the ascendancy internationally, and we wait to see if Australia's live experiment will be rekindled, or taken up elsewhere.

References

Allen Consulting Group. (2005). *Measuring the impact of publicly funded research* (Report to the Australian Government Department of Education, Science and Training). Canberra: Allen Consulting Group.

Austrian Science Fund (FWF)/European Science Foundation (ESF). (2007). *Science impact: Rethinking the impact of basic research on society and the economy*. Retrieved September 18, 2007, from http://www.science-impact.ac.at/index.html

Department of Education, Science and Training (DEST). (2004a). *Backing Australia's ability: Building our future through science and innovation.* Canberra: Commonwealth of Australia.

Department of Education, Science and Training (DEST). (2004b). *Evaluation of knowledge and innovation reforms consultation report.* Canberra: Commonwealth of Australia.

Department of Education, Science and Training (DEST). (2005a). *Research quality framework: Assessing the quality and impact of research in Australia—Advanced approaches paper* (Report by the RQF Expert Advisory Group). Canberra: Commonwealth of Australia.

Department of Education, Science and Training (DEST). (2005b). *Research quality framework: Assessing the quality and impact of research in Australia—Final advice on the preferred RQF model* (Report by the RQF expert advisory group). Canberra: Commonwealth of Australia.

Department of Education, Science and Training (DEST). (2005c). *Research quality framework: Assessing the quality and impact of research in Australia—Issues paper* (RQF expert advisory group). Canberra: Commonwealth of Australia.

Department of Education, Science and Training (DEST). (2005d). *Research quality framework: Assessing the quality and impact of research in Australia—The preferred model* (Report by the RQF expert advisory group). Canberra: Commonwealth of Australia.

Department of Education, Science and Training (DEST). (2006a). *Australian government endorses research quality framework* [Media release]. Retrieved September 18, 2007, from http://www.dest.gov.au/Ministers/Media/Bishop/2006/11/B002141106.asp

Department of Education, Science and Training (DEST). (2006b). *Research quality framework: Assessing the quality and impact of research in Australia—Research impact* (Report by the RQF development advisory group). Canberra: Commonwealth of Australia.

Department of Education, Science and Training (DEST). (2006c). *Research quality framework: Assessing the quality and impact of research in Australia—The recommended RQF* (Report by the RQF development advisory group). Canberra: Commonwealth of Australia.

Department of Education, Science and Training (DEST). (2006d). *RQF guiding principles: Research impact* (Report by the RQF development advisory group). Canberra: Commonwealth of Australia.

Department of Education, Science and Training (DEST). (2007). *Research quality framework: Assessing the quality and impact of research in Australia—RQF submission specifications.* Canberra: Commonwealth of Australia.

Department of Innovation, Industry, Science and Research (IISR). (2007). *Cancellation of Research Quality Framework implementation* [media release]. Retrieved April 22, 2008, from http://minister.industry.gov.au/SenatortheHonKimCarr/Pages/CANCELLATIONOFRESEARCHQUALITYFRAMEWORKIMPLEMENTATION.aspx

Donovan, C. (2006, August). An instrument too blunt to judge sharp minds. *Times Higher Education Supplement,* 14.

Donovan, C. (2007a, May). *Accounting for the triple bottom line: A robust qualitative measure of the public value of research.* Paper presented at the Austrian Science Fund/European Science Foundation Conference on Science Impact: Rethinking the Impact of Basic Research on Society and the Economy, Vienna.

Donovan, C. (2007b). The qualitative future of research evaluation. *Science and Public Policy,* 34(8), 565–574.

Donovan, C. (2007c) Introduction: Future pathways for science policy and research assessment: Metrics vs. peer review, quality vs. impact. *Science and Public Policy,* 34(8), 538–542.

Martin, B. (2007, May). *Assessing the impact of basic research on society and the economy.* Paper presented at the Austrian Science Fund/European Science Foundation Conference on Science Impact: Rethinking the Impact of Basic Research on Society and the Economy, Vienna.

Research Quality Framework Technical Working Group on Research Impact (TWGRI). (2006). *Final report: Optimal methodology for assessing research impact.* Canberra: TWGRI.

Spaapen, J., Dijstelbloem, H., & Wamelink, F. (2007). *Evaluating research in context: A method for comprehensive assessment.* Hague, Netherlands: COS.

Wooding, S., Hanney, S., Buxton, M., & Grant, J. (2004). *The returns from arthritis research, vol. 1: Approach, analysis and recommendations.* Cambridge: RAND Europe.

CLAIRE DONOVAN is a research fellow at the Research Evaluation and Policy Project in the Political Science Program, Research School of Social Sciences, the Australian National University.

Quinlan, K. M., Kane, M., & Trochim, W. M. K. (2008). Evaluation of large research initiatives: Outcomes, challenges, and methodological considerations. In C. L. S. Coryn & M. Scriven (Eds.), *Reforming the evaluation of research. New Directions for Evaluation, 118,* 61–72.

5

Evaluation of Large Research Initiatives: Outcomes, Challenges, and Methodological Considerations

Kathleen M. Quinlan, Mary Kane, William M. K. Trochim

Abstract

The authors synthesize relevant literature and findings of evaluations of four large-scale, federally funded scientific research programs in the United States to identify desired outcomes of these types of programs, major evaluation challenges, and methodological principles and approaches. Evaluators face numerous contextual, political, and methodological challenges in evaluating big science. The authors propose that these may be addressed through participatory planning, such as concept mapping, triangulation of evidence, use of promising methodologies, and a systems approach. © Wiley Periodicals, Inc.

Biomedical research has undergone a significant transformation since the mid-1960s. In the United States, National Institute for Health (NIH) funding has been increasing since 1970 and doubled between 1998 and 2003 (Loscalzo, 2006). Concurrently, the nature, organization, and management of the scientific enterprise have changed (Edgerton, 1999; Nash & Stillman, 2003). Big science is now a significant portion of the NIH

budget (more than $5 million) and is growing in popularity with Congress and the public as a way to call attention to specific health issues.

There are two major types of large-scale scientific research enterprise that stand in contrast to the traditional model of individual investigator-initiated awards. The first, centers of excellence programs, takes a multidisciplinary team approach focused on interaction between basic and clinical researchers to foster translational research. Major goals of center programs include offering more effective support for independently funded investigators, gaining increased attention to a program's research on the part of the center's home institution, recruiting established researchers to the program's area of interest, developing new investigators, expanding education of health professionals and the general public, and demonstrating state-of-the-art prevention, diagnosis, and treatment techniques (Manning, McGeary, Estabrook, & Committee for Assessment of NIH Centers of Excellence Programs, 2004). Research centers have also become popular with the public, advocacy organizations, and Congress, creating political pressure to establish new center programs to address specific diseases. Political interests, though, must be tempered by an understanding of when and how to make the best use of center grants (Manning et al., 2004).

Another type of large research initiative funded by the U.S. government is clinical research networks. Clinical research networks share some of the goals of center programs. However, they are focused on conducting clinical trials, which require coordination between multiple clinical centers, rather than direct interaction between basic and clinical investigators for translational research.

As government expenditures in scientific research have risen, pressure to demonstrate results from these investments also increases (Brainard, 2002a, 2002b; U.S. General Accounting Office, 2000). All government agencies are increasingly called on to demonstrate accountability, exemplified by the Government Performance and Results Act (GPRA) passed in 1993 (U.S. Office of Management and Budget, 1993). This effort led to a standardized governmentwide process for evaluating all federal programs, called the Program Assessment Rating Tool (PART), which, in turn, spawned a Web site for reporting results to the public (www.expectmore.gov). The National Institutes of Health Reform Act of 2006 (U.S. Congress, 2006) emphasized accountability for centers for excellence and included a specific requirement to report biennially on the performance and research outcomes of each center of excellence.

The confluence of these trends necessitates development of ways of evaluating the effectiveness of large-scale publicly funded scientific research enterprises. These large initiatives pose new management and evaluation challenges. The emergence of large initiatives requires assessment of a broader range of outcomes, including the social impact of the research (Smith, 2001). A recent Institute of Medicine report (Nash & Stillman, 2003) emphasizes measuring the technical and scientific output (such as data and research tools), benefits to the field, and the project's management and organizational structure, including staff performance, training, and retention. A 2004 IOM report recommends formal, external, retrospective review on a regular basis—at least every 5 to 7 years (Manning et al., 2004).

This chapter draws on the literature and the authors' experience with four projects to address three major questions on this topic: (1) What are the desired outcomes in large-scale, federally funded U.S. research initiatives?, (2) What are the major challenges in conducting these evaluations?, and (3) What methodologies are suggested by previous work?

Methodology

Using the lens of the three research questions just described, we examine four projects from the authors' portfolio of recent and current work, together with existing literature and documents. In all four projects, we developed an evaluation framework for a major research center program or clinical research networks program. Three of the four projects focus on the evaluation-planning phase of work, consistent with a finding from a 2004 study of 12 federal program evaluations that "the most critical factor in successful implementation of the evaluation design was the thoroughness of the design process" (Howell & Yemane, 2006, p. 234). The four projects are:

1. Centers for Disease Control and Prevention's Prevention Research Centers, or PRCs (Andersen et al., 2006)
2. National Cancer Institute's Transdisciplinary Tobacco Use Research Centers, or TTURCs (Stokols et al., 2003)
3. The National Institute for Allergy and Infectious Disease's Regional Centers of Excellence for Biodefense and Emerging Infectious Diseases Research Program (Concept Systems, 2007)
4. The National Institute for Allergy and Infectious Disease's Division of AIDS clinical research networks (National Institute of Allergy and Infectious Diseases [NIAID], 2006)

Each project used an integrated inquiry approach unified by concept mapping—a mixed-methods, structured group concept mapping methodology. Concept mapping (Trochim, 1989; Kane & Trochim, 2007) is a well-established social research method that combines familiar qualitative processes, such as brainstorming and sorting and rating of ideas with rigorous multivariate statistical analyses to create a shared conceptual framework. Each project involved a diverse range of stakeholders who defined success for their initiative, identified key evaluation questions, and weighed in on approaches that fit their context. The concept-mapping methodology is especially interesting in the context of evaluating large research efforts because it presents a rigorous structured approach that can be used effectively by scientists in the process of articulating the conceptual or logic model that underlies their endeavor—a major challenge in this type of evaluation.

Findings

The findings are organized by the three main research questions. Findings for each question integrate lessons learned from review of the four key projects and related literature.

Desired Outcomes. "Big science" initiatives are intended to achieve complex goals. Improved health outcomes are the ultimate intended impact of the public health research programs studied here. Given the long-term nature of that goal, we must look at the steps in the process that will lead from research to improved health outcomes. Scientific knowledge gained from research must be translated and applied in practice, policy, and service delivery to effect health outcomes. Indeed, a hallmark of center grant initiatives is the focus on translational science. Translating research may involve developing interventions, including prevention or treatment policies and practices or products such as vaccines or therapeutics. It may involve changes in public policy—an important outcome, particularly in the case of tobacco control. Finally, communication, public recognition, and uptake of new prevention and treatment approaches are essential elements in integrating research with practice. Advocacy organizations that lobby for creation of center programs expect the programs will lead to increased public attention to the topic.

Effective translation of scientific knowledge, though, depends on high-quality, strategically focused science. High-quality scientific research is traditionally evidenced by high-quality publications. In these projects, high-quality science involves addressing the most pressing questions with appropriate methods and designs that are feasible and logically connected to the rest of the research agenda. Stakeholders seek innovation in methods, models, technologies, and techniques. Finally, some expect flexibility in the management of the research portfolio, to enable responsiveness to emerging discoveries and scientific needs.

Joint ownership of, leadership for, and coordination of efforts in service of a broad strategic research agenda are particular concerns in these enterprises. Good science has always taken place within a community that shares and builds on prior knowledge, but big science brings the need for coordination of efforts into sharper focus.

Collaboration and coordination emerge as major elements of success across all the programs we studied. For many center grant initiatives, transdisciplinary integration is also a key factor for overall research success, adding a layer of complexity to collaboration.

Collaboration extends to broader communities of interest, which are defined according to the center or network. For instance, the mission of prevention research networks includes engaging community members as partners in applied research. In clinical trials research, respectful relationships with patient communities are critical to successful participant enrollment and retention. In other cases, interaction with local public health agencies is required to ensure community contribution. Community engagement is an important step throughout the research process. Involvement in the early phases of research helps ensure that the most pressing and appropriate questions are included in the research agendas, and it lays the foundation for successful translation and use at the end of a project.

Across the programs we investigated, recruitment of top-notch scientists and training of new investigators in the field are important goals. These efforts are described both as vital to immediate research productivity and important to creating an expanded cadre of experienced researchers in the field to support future advancements in the field. Success also depends on adequate financial resources, which participants in our projects described in two main ways. First, centers and networks seek to leverage resources from other sources, including host institutions, other government sources (noncenter or non-network funds), and industry. Second, typical grants management concerns about time lags, communication between program and accounting staff, and transparency of procedures are magnified with multi-institutional centers and networks. Not only must funding flow smoothly between the NIH and the core institution, but the centers or networks must also establish internal funds management practices that are accountable, transparent, and efficient across institutions.

Some of these large-scale research initiatives are specifically intended to build capacity and infrastructure. For instance, a goal of the Regional Centers of Excellence for Biodefense and Emerging Infectious Diseases Research is to build a web of regional laboratories to support emergency response in the event of an infectious disease emergency. Similarly, stakeholders expect the Prevention Research Centers to be an expert resource that will furnish technical assistance to public health organizations.

Efficient management is vital to success when dealing with the large sums of money, many people, substantial core facilities, and multi-institutional coordination associated with these enterprises. Scientific management has already been mentioned, but operations management is also required. With many centers engaged in similar activities, harmonizing operations and procedures and sharing key resources, including data, are also desirable. Through resource sharing and economies of scale, efficiency, and cost savings are often expected, particularly in the case of clinical research networks (Inventory and Evaluation of Clinical Research Networks, 2006b). Knowledge management is a subtext underlying overt collaboration and management themes.

Finally, our projects highlighted the need for effective management and leadership on the part of the granting agencies, as well as strong relationships between the grantees and the granting agency. Responsibility for success rests with both the grantees and the granting agencies.

Across various center and network research enterprises, there are common desired outcomes. There are also similarities in the pathways to those goals. Nonetheless, each initiative has its own unique purposes, histories, and contexts that must be understood and taken into account in creating a responsive evaluation design.

Challenges. These large biomedical research initiatives pose significant evaluation challenges. First, the long-term nature of scientific research makes it difficult to evaluate because there are various paths from basic research to human benefits (Manning et al., 2004; National Research Council, 1999; National Academy of Sciences, National Academy of Engineering, & Institute of Medicine, 1996, 2001).

As described earlier, these types of grants are designed to expand the human resources available in a field, in part by influencing the career paths of young investigators (Ailes, Roessner, & Feller, 1997). Yet it is difficult and time-consuming to track people over the period of time required to determine impact on career path (Manning et al., 2004).

These programs typically consist of many centers or networks. In our sample, the number of separate centers or networks ranges from 6 to more than 25. Each center or network typically has its own specialty area and operates under local conditions. This variability in context makes it difficult to compare centers or networks within a program meaningfully (Manning et al., 2004). Similarly, if results are aggregated across centers and networks within a program, it is difficult to identify appropriate comparisons or benchmarks at the program level.

In a related vein, although good center and network practices and operations contribute to achievement of positive outcomes, the effectiveness of clinical research networks and centers is also affected by funding agency input (Inventory and Evaluation of Clinical Research Networks, 2006a). Funding agencies must create funding flows, patterns, and support structures that will create conditions for grantee success. This interdependency suggests that an evaluation should be at the level of the enterprise as a whole, including attention to both the grantees and the granting agency. With many organizational layers contributing to the overall success of the enterprise, it is difficult to define the focus, level of detail, and boundaries of an evaluation.

A key question is whether center grant initiatives are a more effective approach to funding scientific research than other grant mechanisms. This question, though important to funding policy, is particularly difficult to answer. One approach is to focus on the unique mission of center grants. Another approach, which is fraught with the assumption of comparability of programs, is to focus on the common denominator of scientific quality and productivity. This second approach is further complicated by the difficulty of separating the effect of a center grant mechanism from other factors, such as highly talented and motivated individual investigators. Furthermore, when leveraging of funds is an explicit goal of a program, it is expected that center research will be supported not only by center funding but by other mechanisms and types of support (Manning et al., 2004; National Academy of Sciences et al., 1996, 2001). Something as simple as attributing a research paper to a particular grant can be difficult when multiple sources of support contributed to its completion. Paradoxically, it is just this type of synergy across researchers; institutions; and physical, financial, and intellectual resources that is a desirable outcome of this type of funding approach and may be at the heart of cost savings and efficiency.

This example illustrates the challenge involved in clarifying the stories we would like to tell about these initiatives. Programs must often balance tensions between competing goals, and this situation is no less so. Being aware of the connections, interdependencies, and tensions among goals is one step in the process of articulating program expectations and designing evaluations that will address them.

Peer review is a touchstone of scientific evaluation and should be incorporated into evaluation of large-scale research programs (Manning et al., 2004; National Academy of Sciences et al., 1996, 2001; Committee on Science, Engineering, and Public Policy, National Academy of Sciences, National Academy of Engineering, & Institute of Medicine, 2000; Committee on Facilitating Interdisciplinary Research, National Academy of Sciences, National Academy of Engineering, Institute of Medicine, & Committee on Science, Engineering, and Public Policy, 2004). However, the size and scope of these research initiatives makes it difficult to find expert peer reviewers who are not involved with the program and do not have a conflict of interest (Manning et al., 2004; National Academy of Sciences et al., 1996, 2001).

Although the challenges described thus far are largely methodological, there are also significant barriers posed by tradition, context, and politics. Traditionally, investigators funded extramurally by the NIH work in academic institutions that have reward structures and evaluation criteria inconsistent with this new approach to scientific funding. A major goal of the big science approach is to cultivate new investigators, but large *collaborative* projects with long-term outcomes are not well rewarded in the individually oriented academic reward structure (Nash & Stillman, 2003). Transdisciplinary interaction, community engagement, and a focus on translational science are also goals that are not well supported by institutions in which researchers work.

Furthermore, substantive evaluation of many facets of the scientific enterprise is new for scientists and stands in contrast to the tradition of academic freedom and intellectual autonomy. Until now, granting agency expectations for accountability have been primarily administrative rather than substantial.

With such large-scale funding, decisions become highly politicized. Funded centers and networks put down roots in a place by virtue of capital investment in infrastructure, a large number of staff, and relationships with local community entities. When core facilities constitute a significant economic force on which a region or an institution depends, questions of its survival become politicized.

Power dynamics are also significant. Principal investigators of these large centers and networks control millions of dollars of funding, have considerable influence over the careers of many colleagues, and enjoy privileged positions in their home institution. They can become such a powerful force in their area of research that the typical power and authority relationship between grantor and grantee may be affected. Appreciating this political backdrop is useful in considering the incentives and disincentives of various stakeholders to participate in an evaluation.

Methodological Considerations. We do not attempt to catalog potential methods or measures here. Instead, we highlight several key themes in the development of this new branch of evaluation practice and illustrate promising approaches on the basis of our experience.

Participation. There are many stakeholders in the evaluation of large-scale scientific research, including federal agency staff, funded investigators and their staff, community members, other scientists, advocacy organizations, industry, and the public at large. To fully understand the program and its desired outcomes and construct meaningful measures that will be feasible to administer, these perspectives must be taken into account. Involving these stakeholders at all stages of the evaluation process helps ensure that the approach has the greatest utility. The example projects all began with a concept mapping process (Trochim, 1989; Kane & Trochim, 2007) that enabled thorough participation in creation of a shared conceptual framework of the expectations of the program. The result in each case was a collaboratively authored concept map that visually depicted participants' views of the success characteristics or outcomes of the program and the relationships among them. The map became the basis for a logic model of the program.

Attention to Consequences. Introducing an evaluation measurement into a system causes changes in practice in the system. In a complex and relatively new system, consequences may be difficult to predict. Therefore, we recommend engaging stakeholders in considering the potential consequences of a measure. Ideally, the evaluation process will help players in the system create conditions for success. Engaging stakeholders in this type of thinking helps to create a positive culture of evaluation.

Promising Methodologies. Across all of these large-scale research initiatives, stakeholders expect high-quality research. In the past few decades, bibliometric analysis has emerged as an important way of illuminating scientific influence and impact. Bibliometrics involves quantitative assessment of scientific publications, the works they cite, and citations of them. Several index variables enable comparison to baseline citation rate in the relevant literature. It builds on the system of peer review established within the scientific community (Osareh, 1996). Bibliometrics were used in the case of the Transdisciplinary Tobacco Utilization Research Centers project (Stokols et al., 2003).

Another emerging approach is use of survey techniques of staff and researchers. In the TTURCs project, the items generated by stakeholders as part of the concept mapping process were the starting point for developing and validating a comprehensive survey that covered the whole range of identified outcome areas (Stokols et al., 2003).

Other researchers (Corley, Melkers, & Johns, 2006; Vonortas & Malerba, 2005; Zuckerman & Kupfer, 2005) have used social network analysis as a tool in evaluating collaboration in these types of research program.

Historically, science has been evaluated by assessing the scientific quality of the work, largely through peer review of research proposals and publications (Jefferson & Godlee, 1999; Kostoff, 1994a, 1994b, 1995). Virtually all recent studies of this topic recommend peer review, with notable enhancements and modifications that take into account the current context of science (Manning et al., 2004; National Academy of Sciences et al., 1996, 2001; Committee on Science, Engineering, and Public Policy et al., 2000; Committee on Facilitating Interdisciplinary Research et al., 2004). The judgments of external, impartial experts with the knowledge and experience to understand the research must be balanced with other sources of data. To evaluate research in progress, the Committee on Science, Engineering, and Public Policy et al. (2000) recommend that experts (both scholars and users) review quantitative data on the basis of the criteria of quality, relevance, and leadership. They further recommend use of a process of international benchmarking (Committee on Science, Engineering, and Public Policy et al., 2000), using a panel of non-U.S. and U.S. experts to assess "the relative position of US research today, the expected relative position of US research in the future, and the key factors influencing relative US performance" (National Academy of Sciences et al., 2001, p. 11). The interdisciplinary focus of many large research initiatives requires inclusion of researchers with interdisciplinary expertise, as well as researchers with expertise in the relevant disciplines (Committee on Facilitating Interdisciplinary Research et al., 2004).

Assembling a Body of Evidence. No single analysis is likely to establish definitively the effects of such complex programs. Therefore designs should incorporate a variety of measures that, taken together, can demonstrate a pattern of results that will enable reasonable causal inference. When more than one type of evidence is gathered for the same construct, as with reports from investigators and site-visit-report and center-profile data, evaluations should cross-check these data sources (Committee on Science, Engineering, and Public Policy et al., 2000). The evaluator, like an attorney, assembles the case so that each piece of evidence is woven together with other pieces of evidence to create a story. Expert panels, as we have described, may be the jury who weighs in on the case, adding their interpretations. The conceptual models of the program, such as the concept-map framework and resulting logic model described earlier, offer a vehicle for integrating results from multiple inquiries.

Systems Approach. Typically, evaluation is done as a single ad hoc event. In contrast, our experience suggests the need for a systems approach to evaluation. A systems approach seeks to build in rigorous evaluation throughout the funding process and life cycle, to ensure a seamless integration with other grant activities and give feedback at key points to inform decision making by various users. There is little precedent for systems approaches to evaluation of large scientific research endeavors (see as exceptions Stokols et al., 2003; and National Academy of Sciences et al., 1996). However, the size, scope, and goals of these large-scale scientific research initiatives suggest this need. Building feedback mechanisms into the life of the grant is philosophically and practically consistent with the funding mechanisms. Doing so also presents the challenge of evaluating the program as a whole, which includes both the funder and the grantees.

Conclusion

Taken together, these four projects enrich our understanding of the U.S. context of the evaluation of large-scale research initiatives. They highlight key questions and outcome domains that specific center programs and clinical research networks must address. They also point to challenges that must be addressed by evaluators.

Evaluators must adjust their role to fit the unique context of scientific research, drawing on their evaluation methodology and research expertise and a rich understanding of the unique evaluation context of scientific research. They must offer expertise in designing an evaluation that is sensitive to the scientific context. They also have to be able to offer assistance and advice in integrating evaluation into existing systems, coordinate and aggregate expert judgments, compare expert judgment to other sources of data that address the same evaluation questions, and help to ensure that the results become part of the feedback to pertinent users in the system.

References

Ailes, C., Roessner, D., & Feller, I. (1997). *The impact on industry of interaction with engineering research centers* (Final report prepared for the National Science Foundation). Arlington, VA: SRI International. Retrieved August 8, 2006, from http://www.sri.com/policy/csted/reports/sandt/erc/

Andersen, L., Gwaltney, M., Sundra, D., Brownson, R., Kane, M., Cross, A., et al. (2006). Using concept mapping to develop a logic model for the prevention research centers program. *Preventing Chronic Disease, 3*(1). Retrieved April 3, 2007, from www.cdc.gov/pcd/issues/2006/jan/05_0153.htm

Brainard, J. (2002a, June 21). New director discusses NIH's massive budget. *Chronicle of Higher Education.* Retrieved June 13, 2007, from http://chronicle.com/weekly/v48/i41/41a02503.htm

Brainard, J. (2002b, March 29). New science measures related by OMB. *Chronicle of Higher Education*. Retrieved June 13, 2007, from http://chronicle.com/weekly/v48/i29/29a02502.htm

Committee on Facilitating Interdisciplinary Research, National Academy of Sciences, National Academy of Engineering, Institute of Medicine, & Committee on Science, Engineering, and Public Policy. (2004). *Facilitating interdisciplinary research*. Washington, DC: National Academies Press.

Committee on Science, Engineering, and Public Policy, National Academy of Sciences, National Academy of Engineering, & Institute of Medicine. (2000). *Experiments in international benchmarking of US research fields*. Washington, DC: National Academies Press.

Concept Systems. (2007). *Development of an evaluation framework for DMID's regional centers of excellence for biodefense and emerging infectious diseases program: Concept mapping summary report*. Ithaca, NY: Concept Systems.

Corley, E., Melkers, J., & Johns, K. (2006, May). *Layered and evolving networks: Innovative evaluation methods for interdisciplinary research in university-based research centers*. Paper presented at Atlanta Conference on S&T Policy, Atlanta.

Edgerton, D. E. H. (1999). Before big science: The pursuit of modern chemistry and physics, 1800–1940. *Annals of Science, 56*(1), 100–107.

Howell, E. M., & Yemane, A. (2006). An assessment of evaluation designs: Case studies of twelve large federal evaluations. *American Journal of Evaluation, 27*(2), 219–236.

Inventory and Evaluation of Clinical Research Networks. (2006a). *Best practices study final report*. Rockville, MD: WESTAT.

Inventory and Evaluation of Clinical Research Networks. (2006b). *Core and descriptive survey final report*. Rockville, MD: WESTAT.

Jefferson, T., & Godlee, F. (1999). *Peer review in health sciences*. London: British Medical Journal Publishing Group.

Kane, M., & Trochim, W. M. K. (2007). *Concept mapping for planning and evaluation*. Thousand Oaks, CA: Sage.

Kostoff, R. N. (1994a). Assessing research impact—Federal peer-review practices. *Research Evaluation, 18*(1) 31–40.

Kostoff, R. N. (1994b). Quantitative qualitative federal research impact evaluation practice. *Technological Forecasting and Social Change, 45*(2), 189–205.

Kostoff, R. N. (1995). Research requirements for research impact assessment. *Research Policy, 24*(6), 869–882.

Loscalzo, J. (2006). NIH-sponsored clinical trials worth the cost, Reuters Health Information: The NIH budget and the future of biomedical research. *New England Journal of Medicine, 354*(16), 1665–1667.

Manning, F. G., McGeary, M., Estabrook, R., & Committee for Assessment of NIH Centers of Excellence Programs. (2004). *National Institute of Health extramural center programs: Criteria for initiation and evaluation*. Washington, DC: Institute of Medicine, Board on Health Sciences Policy.

Nash, S. J., & Stillman, B. W. (2003). *Large-scale biomedical science: Exploring strategies for future research*. Washington, DC: National Academies Press.

National Academy of Sciences, National Academy of Engineering, & Institute of Medicine. (1996). *An assessment of the National Science Foundation's science and technology centers program*. Washington, DC: National Academies Press.

National Academy of Sciences, National Academy of Engineering, & Institute of Medicine. (2001). *Implementing the Government Performance and Results Act for research: A status report*. Washington, DC: National Academies Press.

National Institute of Allergy and Infectious Diseases (NIAID). (2006). *NIAID announces leadership for newly restructured HIV/AIDS clinical trials networks, 2006*. Retrieved August 17, 2006, from http://www3.niaid.nih.gov/news/newsreleases/2006/leadership.htm

National Research Council. (1999). *Evaluating federal research programs: Research and the Government Performance and Results Act*. Washington, DC: National Academies Press.

Osareh, F. (1996). Bibliometrics, citation analysis and co-citation analysis: A review of literature. *Libri, 46*(3), 149–158.

Smith, R. (2001). Measuring the social impact of research: Difficult but necessary. *British Medical Journal, 323*, 528.

Stokols, D., Fuqua, J., Gress, J., Harvey, R., Phillips, K., Baezconde-Garbanati, L., et al. (2003). Evaluating transdisciplinary science. *Nicotine and Tobacco Research, 5*, S-1, S21–S39.

Trochim, W. (1989). An introduction to concept mapping for planning and evaluation. In W. Trochim (Ed.), *Special Issue of Evaluation and Program Planning, 12*, 1–16.

U.S. Congress. (2006). *National Institutes of Health Reform Act of 2006. 109th Cong., H.R. 6164*. Retrieved March 9, 2007, from http://www.govtrack.us/congress/billtext.xpd?bill=h109–6164

U.S. General Accounting Office. (2000). *NIH research: Improvements needed in monitoring external grants* (GAO-HEHS-AIMD-00–139). Washington, DC: U.S. General Accounting Office.

U.S. Office of Management and Budget. (1993). *Government Performance Results Act of 1993. Executive Office of the President of the United States, 1993*. Retrieved August 17, 2006, from http://www.whitehouse.gov/omb/mgmt-gpra/gplaw2m.html

Vonortas, N. S., & Malerba, F. (2005, October). *Using social network methodology to evaluate research and development programs*. Paper presented at the joint conference of the Canadian Evaluation Society and the American Evaluation Association, Toronto, Ontario.

Zuckerman, B. L., & Kupfer, L. (2005, October). *Social network-based design of collaborative research program evaluation*. Paper presented at the joint conference of the Canadian Evaluation Society and the American Evaluation Association, Toronto, Ontario.

KATHLEEN M. QUINLAN *is director of research and a senior consultant at Concept Systems.*

MARY KANE *is president and chief executive officer of Concept Systems.*

WILLIAM M. K. TROCHIM *is professor of policy analysis and management at Cornell University, where he is also director of evaluation for extension and outreach.*

NEW DIRECTIONS FOR EVALUATION • DOI: 10.1002/ev

Gray, D. O. (2008). Making team science better: Applying improvement-oriented evaluation principles to evaluation of cooperative research centers. In C. L. S. Coryn & M. Scriven (Eds.), *Reforming the evaluation of research. New Directions for Evaluation, 118,* 73–87.

6

Making Team Science Better: Applying Improvement-Oriented Evaluation Principles to Evaluation of Cooperative Research Centers

Denis O. Gray

Abstract

The rise of the research center has changed the landscape of U.S. research enterprise. It has also created a number of evaluation challenges, particularly when considering strategically focused, multifaceted cooperative research centers (CRCs). The author argues that although recent CRC evaluation efforts have gone a long way toward meeting the needs of groups interested in accountability, they do little to meet the needs of inexperienced scientist managers who try to lead and manage these organizationally complex initiatives. An exception to this trend is described: the improvement-oriented evaluation *strategy pioneered by the National Science Foundation IUCRC program.* © Wiley Periodicals, Inc.

Note: The material in this paper is based on work supported by the STC program (under agreement no. CHE-9876674) and the IUCRC program (under agreement no. IIP0631414) of the National Science Foundation.

" **A**lthough accountability will continue to be an important purpose for program evaluation," write Newcomer, Hatry, and Wholey, "the major goal should be to improve program performance . . . when program evaluation is used only for external accountability purposes and does not help managers improve their programs, the results are often not worth the cost of the evaluation" (1994, p. 2).

Research Centers

Perhaps no single development has changed the landscape of research funding and operations in the United States more than the rise of the research center. At a fundamental level, a center (or lab or institute) is simply an organized research unit, one that is typically multidisciplinary and team-based (Friedman & Friedman, 1986). Centers have existed for quite some time, but funding for such ventures has gone from a small-scale curiosity to a major component of the research budget for such organizations as the National Science Foundation (NSF), National Institute of Health (NIH), and other federal agencies over the past several decades (Coburn, 1995). For instance, NSF currently supports nine separate center-funding initiatives totaling more than $260 million and recently announced a new Undergraduate Research Centers initiative (National Science Foundation, 2005). NIH boasts an even greater number of center-based initiatives in its Roadmap for Medical Research (National Institute of Health, 2006). Federally funded research and development centers (FFRDCs), research and development (R&D) performing organizations administered by industrial, academic, or other nonprofit organizations for the federal government such as the National Center for Atmospheric Research at the University of Colorado or Lincoln Labs at MIT, now receive a staggering $5.6 billion in federal funding (National Science Foundation, 2007). However, these high-profile centers are just the tip of the proverbial iceberg. According to the *Research Centers and Services Directory* (2006), there are more than 14,000 university-based and nonprofit research centers in the United States and Canada and more than 27,500 worldwide.

From an evaluation perspective, research centers and "team science" (Gray, 2007) are interesting for reasons beyond their growth and sheer numbers. First, because they have been subject to evaluative scrutiny for some time, they constitute a basis for judging where research evaluation can, and perhaps should, go in the future. Second, because they are more complicated and multifaceted than most "traditional" research initiatives, they present some unique evaluation challenges. Finally, because centers are not only multifaceted, but also organizationally complex, they raise the profile of an important, but rarely mentioned, evaluation stakeholder group: local center management.

Center Evaluation Issues

Over the years, centers have grown in number and in terms of their share of the federal R&D budget, in large part, because policy makers and science and technology (S&T) scholars alike believe larger scale, team-based, multidisciplinary, strategically focused, and multifaceted research initiatives are more likely to produce high-value, high-impact research than traditional individual principal investigator (PI) awards. However, because of their instrumental nature, these initiatives have not operated under the system of benign self-regulation more traditional research schemes face.

A good case in point is evaluation of various cooperative research center (CRC) initiatives. CRCs are university-based, multidisciplinary organized research units (that is, they are not part of academic departments) that are designed to promote interaction with, and knowledge and technology transfer to, outside groups, such as industry, government agencies, and even nonprofits, and in the long run they support such goals as enhanced competitiveness, economic development, and improved student education. CRC-type centers are supported by a variety of government agencies and units, notably NSF, the Department of Defense (DOD), the Defense Advanced Research Projects Agency (DARPA), NIH, the National Institute of Standards and Technology (NIST), and state governments (Coburn, 1995). Because such centers were somewhat controversial when first introduced (National Science Foundation, 1984), they have been the focus of evaluation oversight for more than two decades (Cohen, Florida, & Goe, 1994; Feller, 1997).

Because of their complex and organizationally mediated nature, CRCs also present some unique evaluation challenges. To understand these challenges better, consider a brief description of a not-atypical CRC.

The Center for Environmentally Responsible Solvents and Processes (CERSP) is an NSF-funded Science and Technology Center managed by the University of North Carolina, Chapel Hill. CERSP's vision is to enable a revolution in sustainable technology through cutting-edge integrated physical science and engineering, social science, and an educational program. CERSP includes four additional university partners. Although its core research program in chemistry and chemical engineering is diverse and includes both basic and more applied studies, it also supports a social science program on innovation issues. To achieve its goal, it supports 39 faculty, 79 graduate, and 68 undergraduate students per year. It attempts to promote technology transfer to industry via affiliated industrial consortia and other boundary spanning centers. To achieve its educational goals, it has initiated curricular changes for graduate students and holds a weekly multicampus teleconference meeting and innovation seminar. To achieve its outreach mission, it manages a K–12 STEM initiative and an undergraduate research program aimed at underrepresented undergraduates at a nearby HBCU.

NEW DIRECTIONS FOR EVALUATION • DOI: 10.1002/ev

Given such a research venture, one set of evaluation challenges relates to the complexity of the center's research portfolio and missions. To meet the needs of program sponsors, the evaluator must grapple with complicating questions: How can I evaluate the merit of a diverse portfolio of projects that may range from basic to applied? When and how can I measure downstream benefits and impacts of a multiyear research effort to a diffuse group of potential beneficiaries? How do I evaluate educational and other nonresearch benefits?

An additional set of evaluation challenges exists because CRCs tend to be relatively complex autonomous (or semiautonomous) organizational entities that must run efficiently and effectively to produce intended benefits. For a CRC to be successful, its management must formulate and execute a coherent research strategy, secure and manage funding from multiple sponsors, promote effective "team-science" ("Who'd Want to Work in a Team?" 2003) among multiple internal (university, center, faculty, student) and external (federal, industry, state) stakeholder groups, and manage the research and personnel transitions that are inevitable in a multiyear effort. In short, leadership, organizational, and management execution can make or break a center. However, evaluating the capabilities and performance of a CRC in these domains is not a trivial undertaking. Further, because the burden of managing these complex structures tends to fall on the shoulders of scientists with little or no managerial background or experience (Gray & Walters, 1998), it raises another issue: To what extent has the evaluation community been looking out for the needs of local center directors, a vitally important stakeholder group?

In the next section, I summarize and update the results of a recent review and critique of evaluations of four prominent NSF CRC programs: Industry/University Cooperative Research Centers (IUCRCs), State IUCRCs, Engineering Research Centers, and Science and Technology Centers (Gray, 2000). Consistent with a "utilization-focused evaluation" perspective (Patton, 1997), this review attempts to highlight key evaluation uses (judgment, improvement, knowledge) and key stakeholders. The purpose of this review is twofold: first, to identify the kinds of center evaluation strategies and methods that might be feasible for more traditional research activities; and second, to understand the extent to which these past efforts have truly addressed the evaluation needs of various stakeholder groups. The chapter will then turn to highlighting an "improvement-oriented" evaluation effort that appears to be unique in attempting to meet the needs of local center managers.

Evaluation of Cooperative Research Center

Notwithstanding the challenges just described, by almost any standard, evaluations of CRCs have been ambitious, set a high standard for research evaluation in general, and done a good job of meeting the needs of most

NEW DIRECTIONS FOR EVALUATION • DOI: 10.1002/ev

stakeholder groups. For my purposes, these efforts can be put into three categories: ex ante, outcome, and interim evaluations (Gray, 2000).

Ex Ante Evaluations. Ex ante evaluations take place before the research (or program) commences and are often pivotal to the funding decision (OECD, 1987). For traditional research activities, ex ante evaluation usually involves one-time, traditional scientific peer review by the agency at the project level of analysis. Because CRCs involve bundles of research projects, multiple dimensions of merit, and multiyear funding, CRC ex ante evaluations have moved away from traditional project-level peer review.

In recognition of the more complex and multifaceted nature of CRCs, NSF programs have typically opted for a modified ex ante peer review evaluation. Though still qualitative and judgment-based, these reviews include nonscientific rating dimensions, such as the quality of a center's strategic research plan, the potential for technological or economic success, and managerial excellence. Not surprisingly, given these criteria, the "peer" group for these reviews would typically include industrial scientists, educational experts, economists, and social scientists. In the case of the now-defunct State IUCRC program, a multistage review was used that required state endorsement (and financial commitment) based exclusively on economic development criteria before a scientific and technological review could take place within NSF. Internally, most centers also use a similar modified multicriteria peer-review process to make decisions about individual (or bundles of) research projects (Steenhuis & Gray, 2005). The composition of the review committees varies from program to program with external review committees (ERCs) and standing review committees (STCs) soliciting feedback from an external advisory committee that includes outside academic and industrial scientists and the IUCRC relying primarily on industry assessments. Though modest evaluation innovations, these methods appear to give both agency representatives and center managers more flexible tools to judge the quality of diverse and explicitly instrumental research agendas.

Outcome Evaluations. Outcome evaluations focus on examining the extent to which various proximal or distal outcomes or the impact of CRCs have been achieved (OECD, 1987; Mathison, 2005). As other authors in this volume have discussed, outcome evaluations of traditional research activities are rare and, when done, typically focus exclusively on scientific impact via bibliometric impact assessments. In contrast, outcome evaluations of CRCs have been relatively common and ambitious, addressing a variety of outcomes and involving relatively sophisticated social science methodologies and tools.

Virtually all CRC outcome evaluations have been ad hoc, program-level evaluation studies conducted by outside evaluation experts, sometimes commissioned or required by some congressional or government oversight group (see, for example, National Research Council, 1988). As a group, these studies have tended to focus on technology transfer outcomes to industry, but they also involve assessments of scientific impact and collateral outcomes, such as educational benefits for graduate students (Ailes, Roessner, & Feller, 1997). From a measurement perspective, these studies have been relatively sophisticated and involved attempts to collect reliable and valid data from critical stakeholders, such as industry sponsors, program graduates, or student employers on attitudes, perceptions, and activities and follow-up data on outcomes through well-designed questionnaires and interviews. As another methodological plus, most of these assessments have involved population surveys of all known stakeholders.

On the other hand, CRC outcome studies have been less sophisticated from an analysis and design standpoint. Many of the studies have been very multivariate, but most analyses have involved univariate or bivariate descriptions of processes or outcomes by various groups or conditions. Further, as with other areas of research evaluation (Jaffe, 1998), when it comes to answering the question, "Does this program really make a difference (compared to no program or an alternative one)?" most studies have been inferentially weak. There have been some rare exceptions (Roessner, 2000), but few of these studies have included comparison to defensible control groups or even to accepted objective norms. Notwithstanding these quibbles, this collection of assessments has given policy makers and the scholarly community a detailed understanding of the dynamics and outcomes of various CRC initiatives.

Interim Evaluations. Interim evaluations are assessments that occur while the research (or program) is being carried out (OECD, 1987). They typically focus on program inputs and processes, such as managerial performance and research execution, and can include assessments of outputs and proximal outcomes. They range from relatively simple monitoring efforts to formative evaluations and more analytically intensive process evaluations (Rossi, Lipsey, & Freeman, 2004). Gibbons and Georghiou (OECD, 1987) have suggested that such evaluations are most useful when the research enterprise is complex and involves multiple interfaces. Rare for traditional, time-limited research activities, interim evaluations have been relatively common for the more complex and organizationally mediated CRCs. For instance, all of the NSF CRCs considered in my review supported monitoring systems for interim evaluation (Gray, 2000). These systems varied in their comprehensiveness but typically included annual collection of data on inputs (for example, level and type of financial support), operations (number and type of personnel, meetings held), activities (courses offered), and outputs, such as publications and patents. Agency representatives use these data at the program level of analysis to respond to various oversight groups or at the center level of analysis to make interim assessments on center operations and performance.

Surprisingly, with the exception of the IUCRC evaluation effort, which I will describe shortly, the bedrock for most CRC process evaluations has been the same approach used for ex ante evaluation: modified peer review.

For instance, ERCs and STCs (and most CRCs run by other federal agencies) are subject to annual site visit-based evaluations by a team of NSF staff and a group of outside peer reviewers. Drawing primarily on quantitative information found in the monitoring system, qualitative information presented in center reports and information available in presentations made during the site visit, the outside review team prepares a written report summarizing its evaluation of the center to NSF. This process gives agency representatives a basis for judging a center's scientific and managerial progress. It also extends to center management some developmental feedback on their strengths and weaknesses.

Summary. Passage of the Government Performance and Results Act (GPRA) in 1993 increased the urgency of reforming the way we evaluate government research efforts (Cozzens, 2000). Extant evaluations of CRCs appear to demonstrate that evaluations of research can move beyond simple peer reviews in both small and in significant ways. Though modest on its face, use of a modified peer-review process in both ex ante and interim evaluations demonstrates that the research enterprise can be evaluated on the basis of nonscientific criteria and by a peer community that includes industrial scientists, economists, and economic development specialists. This is not a trivial development and is now widely accepted within the broader CRC community.

With respect to outcome evaluations, even though there is still room for improvement, CRC outcome evaluations demonstrate that rigorous social science methods can be used to furnish policy makers with evidence about scientific and nonscientific outcomes, such as technology transfer, commercialization, economic development, and educational impacts. Whether such methods should be applied widely to all types of research is a different question.

Extant CRC evaluation efforts appear to go a long way toward beginning to meet the needs of policy makers and agency representatives to make judgments about programs and centers; they appear to be both much less ambitious and sophisticated in attempting to meet the needs of the other major stakeholder group we have discussed: center directors. Though annual site visit-based modified peer reviews may offer some value to this group, these interim evaluations appear to fall short of meeting the evaluation needs of the relatively inexperienced scientist-managers who are being asked to lead these complex boundary-spanning organizations in very dynamic scientific and technical domains. It is worth noting that a recent and comprehensive report on research evaluation (Ruegg & Feller, 2003) is also silent on this topic.

Fortunately, the broader evaluation community is not silent on this issue. In the next sections, I discuss a strategy—"improvement-oriented" evaluation—designed to meet such needs and constitute an example of this approach with a long-running CRC program.

Improvement-Oriented Evaluation

According to Patton (1997), evaluations can serve three ends: rendering judgments, facilitating improvements, and generating knowledge. He also asserts that evaluation should be judged by its utility in meeting these ends and actual use by various stakeholder groups (Patton, 1997). By this standard, CRC evaluations appear to have done a pretty good job of meeting the needs of agency managers who are concerned with judging or defending the merit of their research allocations and assessing the extent to which those investments have produced intended benefits. They also appear to have done a good job of meeting the policy and scholarly community's need to better understand the dynamics of cooperative research (see Feller, 1997). However, like most program managers, CRC directors tend to be less interested in evaluation for judgment or pure knowledge and more interested in evaluation for improvement. But what does improvement evaluation look like?

Patton (1997) has probably given the fullest and best definition of improvement-oriented evaluation (IOE) in *Utilization-Focused Evaluation*. According to Patton, IOE is a form of evaluation that stresses making things better. It can encompass a variety of approaches, including "formative evaluation, quality enhancement, responsive evaluation, learning organization approaches, humanistic evaluation and Total Quality Management (TQM), among others" (Patton, 1997, p. 68). IOE can use formative evaluation methods, but the two are not the same. Formative evaluation usually involves collecting data just during the start-up or pilot phase of a project to improve implementation. However, true IOE typically involves "using monitoring systems and data collection procedures over time to provide feedback for refining a well-established program" (p. 69). He adds that it usually involves "gathering varieties of data about strengths and weaknesses with the expectation that both will be found and each can be used to inform an ongoing cycle of reflection and innovation" (Patton, 1997, p. 69).

Improvement-Oriented Evaluation Applied to CRCs

Examples of IOE have been presented in the literature for educational and social programs (Patton, 1997). I describe how this strategy has been successfully applied to CRCs.

IUCRC Program. The NSF IUCRC program has been in existence for nearly 30 years (Gray & Walters, 1998). Like other CRCs, the program's most important goal is to develop and transfer new knowledge and technology to industry; it also attempts to enhance graduate education. In contrast to many highly funded center programs discussed in the literature, NSF attempts to achieve this end by way of very modest cost sharing (about $75,000 a year per site) for up to 10 years. Ultimately, NSF hopes to create self-sustaining centers.

NEW DIRECTIONS FOR EVALUATION • DOI: 10.1002/ev

A detailed description of the IUCRC model can be found elsewhere (Gray & Walters, 1998). In brief, IUCRCs are university-based, industrial research consortia. The research performed in the centers tends to be strategic or preproprietary fundamental research and is carried out primarily by faculty and graduate students. IUCRCs follow a relatively standardized set of policies and procedures; members pay an annual fee (usually between $30,000 and $50,000 per year), and they get equal access to, and ownership of, all research and intellectual property, findings, know-how, and technology are transmitted through a variety of means, including periodic reports and semiannual meetings; and members get one vote on the center's Industrial Advisory Board (IAB).

The IUCRC program currently supports 39 centers that involve about 80 universities, about 650 firms, 550 faculty, 600 graduate students, and 200 undergraduate students (Gray & Rivers, 2007). Centers tend to be diverse in terms of budget ($400,000 to $7 million), number of research personnel (5 to 50), and number of industry members (8 to 40). Centers also represent diverse areas of technology: manufacturing, nano- and microtechnology, chemical processing, biotechnology, and advanced electronics, to name a few.

To be successful, an IUCRC director must balance a number of sometimes conflicting requirements and expectations. Specifically, the IUCRC director must attract at least $300,000 in membership support to meet NSF requirements; implement a research program that is industrially relevant and delivers some knowledge transfer or related benefits (for example, well-trained future employees) to keep and expand industry support; make sure that most of its research is "thesis and dissertation quality" and results in quality publications so as to meet university and NSF expectations and to keep faculty happy and committed; and attract additional competitive funding from other federal and state agencies to grow beyond the subsistence level furnished by NSF and industry support. The IUCRC evaluation effort was designed to help center directors successfully address these conflicting demands.

IUCRC Evaluation Effort. The IUCRC Evaluation effort was initiated when the program was first formalized in 1981, and although it has evolved over time, it always embraced IOE principles. Patton (1997) suggests that on the surface, IOE often looks a lot like traditional judgment-oriented evaluation. This has been the case for the IUCRC evaluation, which structurally looks like a relatively traditional, if multifaceted, evaluation effort. Monitoring data are collected on issues such as personnel, budgets, and outputs such as intellectual property (IP) events. Process and outcome data are collected via questionnaires, interviews, and direct observation, generally on an annual basis. An outside evaluation group, the IUCRC Evaluation Team based at North Carolina State University, is responsible for supplying NSF with programwide analyses and summaries.

From an IOE perspective, the most significant change in the IUCRC evaluation effort was the decision by NSF program managers and evaluators to make program improvement a central objective of the evaluation effort (Tornatzky, 1982). Initially, this focus was implicit and was justified by an assumption that "good or even great science was a necessary but not sufficient condition for IUCRC success." More recently, the primacy of improvement has been formalized in a statement of three evaluation objectives: to document IUCRC outcomes and accomplishments for centers and NSF IUCRC; to promote continuous improvement by giving actionable, data-based feedback, analysis, and advice to the centers and NSF; and to identify and communicate programwide best practices.

When form follows function in an evaluation effort, a focus on improvement tends to change what data are collected, how they are collected, and how they are used—and, perhaps most important, the locus and role of the evaluator. Here are major features of the IUCRC evaluation effort that reinforce its focus on center-level improvement.

On-site Evaluator. The major structural innovation in the IUCRC evaluation effort, and the feature that enables it to move from a focus on judgment to improvement, is provision for an on-site evaluator. This person is supported by NSF's award and is responsible for executing a standardized evaluation protocol at the local center and, subsequently, submitting data to the IUCRC evaluation team for national aggregation and analysis. The evaluator is usually an applied social scientist from the host university, but to promote a reasonable level of objectivity, he or she cannot have direct association with the academic unit that operates the center. By committing to an on-site evaluator, the IUCRC evaluation effort was able the address the significant differences that inevitably exist when establishing centers in fields as divergent as child injury prevention science and plasma and lasers in advanced manufacturing. More important, an on-site evaluator enables one to take a local utilization focus, use improvement-oriented instruments and methods, and fundamentally alter the evaluator's role.

Utilization Focus. Although much of the evaluation effort is managed nationally by the IUCRC evaluation team, by locating the evaluator at each center and having the person report to the center director, the IUCRC evaluation effort has attempted to reinforce the primacy of the center director as the main user of the evaluation. As the evaluation protocol evolved over the years, the center director, through his or her interactions with the local evaluator, influenced the focus and content of the evaluation and, consequently, his or her investment in it. This enhances the personal factor, which Patton asserts is the single greatest predictor of evaluation utilization (Patton, 1997).

Improvement-Oriented Assessment Tools and Methods. Consistent with Patton's suggestions, the assessment strategies used in the IUCRC evaluation tend to resemble those used in formative evaluation and TQM.

NEW DIRECTIONS FOR EVALUATION • DOI: 10.1002/ev

In formative evaluation, the evaluator often collects qualitative data about program operations and their implementation. Because the IUCRC evaluator is inside the center and participates in key meetings attended by other stakeholders, he or she has a unique opportunity to operate as a participant-observer. This role is formalized within the IUCRC evaluation by giving the evaluator a structured guide for collecting data and making observations about key operational domains, including the research program, institutional support, operational issues, personnel, and so on. The evaluator prepares a report that covers these issues and submits it first to the director and, subsequently, to NSF.

More important, from an IOE perspective, the evaluator's participant-observer role is an opportunity to generate "real-time reconnaissance" on emerging problems. Over time, evaluators have produced critical information about industry members who expressed dissatisfaction over some aspect of center management or felt that technical or other needs weren't being met; and about faculty members who felt they were being asked to sacrifice quality for expedience. By receiving feedback quickly and informally on these issues from the evaluator, directors have an opportunity to correct problems before serious harm is done (such as loss of a member).

Consistent with a TQM philosophy, the structured assessment activities focus on customers (industry) and suppliers (faculty researchers), self-evaluation, and continuous improvement (Mehrota, 2006). The main tool in this domain is the IUCRC process and outcome survey. In essence, these instruments are annually administered reputability assessments (Rossi, Lipsey, & Freeman, 2004) that collect both objective and subjective feedback from industry and faculty related to key operational and outcome issues, such as perception of and satisfaction with the research program (quality and relevance) and center management practices (communications, strategy); strength and weaknesses; research and commercialization changes (for industry); and publications (for faculty). Because the same data are collected at all centers and aggregated by the IUCRC evaluation project team, directors receive the kind of benchmark-based comparisons that have been demonstrated to improve performance and help identify best practices (Tornatzky, 2001). Evaluators also collect "exit interviews" from firms that decide to leave the center.

Developmental Evaluator. Rossi, Lipsey, and Freeman (2004) suggest that one advantage of an internal evaluator is the ability to "engage in the consultation, education and dialogue required to maximize results" (p. 154). As a capstone to its IOE, the IUCRC evaluation effort tries to optimize this advantage by encouraging the evaluator to become an advisor or consultant to the director (Gray & Walters, 1998). Patton (1997) defines individuals who fill such a role as developmental evaluators, "evaluators who become part of the program design team or an organization's management team" and are "involved in improving the intervention and use evaluative approaches to facilitate ongoing, program, project, product, staff and organizational development" (p. 104).

Armed with the data and information furnished by their assessment activities, insights derived from operating as insider participant-observer for a number of years, and increasingly multiple evaluation assignments, the IUCRC evaluator is typically quite prepared to serve in this role. However, the IUCRC evaluation effort has tried to support the developmental evaluator role in additional ways. First, evaluators meet twice each year, once with directors and once alone, to discuss program issues and share best practices. At a program level, evaluators contribute to, and benefit from, a published volume of best practices (Gray & Walters, 1998).

Costs and Benefits of Using IOE with CRCs

There are certainly risks and problems associated with pursuing an IOE strategy, particularly one that tilts strongly toward developmental evaluation. First and foremost is the difficulty associated with managing the role conflicts inherent in meeting NSF's and the center's needs while trying to serve as an objective data-based evaluator, as well as a management team member and finally an organizational development specialist. As some evidence for role conflict, note that roughly half the IUCRC organizational charts in circulation show the evaluator reporting to NSF, while other charts show evaluators reporting to directors. Evaluators frequently have to grapple with issues of "going native" and forgetting that they are more than members of the team, or forgetting how to resolve ethical issues surrounding confidentiality of some data or conversation and the director's IOE need to know. On a more methodological issue, annual collection of survey data from key participants has resulted in some "questionnaire fatigue" causing the IUCRC evaluation team to reevaluate the protocol and abbreviate some of its formal survey work.

On the other hand, there would appear to be at least three benefits that accrue from taking an IOE approach to the IUCRC program: local center directors actually appear to be using the results; in a number of cases, it appears to lead to a longer-standing, broader commitment to evaluation; and there appears to be a positive effect on the program.

If the acid test for a utilization-focused evaluation approach is use of evaluation findings, the IUCRC appears to have passed that test. Though purely anecdotally, evaluators report countless examples where directors use evaluation data, reconnaissance, and advice to make changes and improve their centers. Benchmarked survey feedback data highlight shortcomings in a center's research agenda or operational problems, such as ineffective IP procedures, and allow the director to take corrective action before significant industry defections resulted. Information obtained via participant observation helps highlight and sometimes resolve festering conflicts between faculty involved in multiuniversity centers that threatened to tear a partnership apart.

Patton (1997) suggests that when evaluation is participatory and collaborative, as the IUCRC effort has tried to be, it "can lead to an ongoing, longer-term commitment to using evaluation logic and building a culture of learning in a program or organization" (p. 100). There is ample evidence that this has been the case for the IUCRC evaluation. For instance, a multistage ex ante project evaluation technique based on nominal group principles developed by evaluators (Level of Interest and Feedback Evaluation, or LIFE) has become so ingrained in the ethos of the program that directors typically manage its implementation completely by themselves. Directors endorsed and cooperated in a series of ambitious process and outcome studies over the years, many of them theses and dissertations, on various issues including industry retention, organizational commitment among faculty, leadership, and student outcomes. In an earlier paper, I reported how a group of "graduating" (no longer funded) IUCRC directors lobbied NSF to continue funding the evaluation effort (Gray, 1997); this has been repeated several times. Although this could be dismissed as simply spending other people's money, some directors budget for an evaluator in new grants or continue to fund the evaluator out of their own funds.

In the final analysis, one could argue that the value of IOE should be judged on how well the IUCRC program and local centers perform. Unfortunately, the attribution problems involved in trying to link IOE with the IUCRC performance would be legion. Nonetheless, it is worth noting some IUCRC outcome metrics. The IUCRC program has just passed its 25th anniversary and is responsible for launching 110 centers, many of them still in operation. It appears to be one of the most heavily leveraged R&D program funded by the federal government, if not the most leveraged. For every dollar that NSF invests in the program, other sources including industry invest about 10 dollars. This feat has been accomplished by a collection of relatively inexperienced scientist-managers, with NSF investing about $130,000 per year in a two-university IUCRC—less than the typical individual NSF PI award. The cost of the onsite evaluation for such a center is $13,000 per year. Ninety percent of member firms indicate they are either "quite" or "very" satisfied with the technical quality of the IUCRC research (Gray & Rivers, 2007), while NSF has just published its second compendia of technology breakthroughs attributed to IUCRC research by member firms (Scott, 2007). These accomplishments helped the IUCRC program receive the Technology Transfer Society's Justin Morril Award for Institutional Excellence in Technology Transfer. The level of impact is unclear, but I believe the IUCRC program's commitment to IOE deserves some of the credit for this success.

With the impetus of GPRA, the evaluation community's focus easily turns to meeting the needs of external stakeholders, such as the oversight groups that are looking for an economic payoff from an applied research initiative or the taxpayers who ultimately support the growing number of state-funded initiatives. However, as we consider how to reform the evaluation of research, we need to recognize that new models of doing research create stakeholder groups that never existed before. The advent of team science changes research from a primarily individualistic enterprise to a complex, organizationally mediated enterprise and creates a new and important internal stakeholder in the process: the scientist-manager who is being asked to lead these ambitious efforts. Fortunately, on the basis of the IUCRC evaluation experience, it appears that an investment in IOE may go a long way toward beginning to meet this group's needs. Hopefully, as interest in and resources for research evaluation increase, the S&T policy community and agency directors will become convinced that evaluation for improvement can go hand in hand with evaluation for accountability.

References

Ailes, C. P., Roessner, D. J., & Feller, I. (1997). *The impact of industry interaction with engineering research centers.* Arlington, VA: SRI International.

Coburn, C. (1995). Partnerships: A compendium of state and federal cooperative technology programs. Columbus, OH: Battelle.

Cohen, W., Florida, R., & Goe, W. R. (1994). *University-industry research centers in the United States.* Pittsburgh, PA: Carnegie Mellon University.

Cozzens, S. E. (2000). Assessing federally supported academic research in the United States. *Research Evaluation, 8*(1), 41–46.

Feller, I. (1997). Technology transfer from universities. In J. C. Smart (Ed.), *Higher education: Handbook of theory and research,* XII (pp. 1–43). New York: Agathon Press.

Friedman, R. S., & Friedman, R. C. (1986). *Sponsorship, organization and program change at 100 universities.* Park, PA: Institute for Policy Research and Evaluation, Pennsylvania State University.

Gray, D. O. (1997). Establishing systemwide evaluations: Program-centered evaluation and the National Science Foundation's industry-university cooperative research centers. In P. Shapira & J. Youtie (Eds.), *Manufacturing modernization: Learning from evaluation practices and results* (pp. 241–250). Atlanta: Georgia Tech University.

Gray, D. O. (2000). Government-sponsored industry-university cooperative research: An analysis of cooperative research center evaluation approaches. *Research Evaluation, 9*(1), 56–67.

Gray, D. O. (2007, February). *Team science: Analyzing the interactions and outcomes.* Paper presented at the meeting of the American Association for the Advancement of Sciences, San Francisco.

Gray, D. O., & Rivers, D. (2007). *National Science Foundation industry-university cooperative research centers: Analysis of 2005–6 structural information.* Washington, DC: North Carolina State University.

Gray, D. O., & Walters, S. G. (Eds.). (1998). *Managing the industry/university cooperative research center: A guide for directors and other stakeholders.* Columbus, OH: Battelle Press.

Jaffe, A. B. (1998). Measurement issues. In L. M. Branscomb & J. Keller (Eds.), *Investing in innovation: Creating a research and innovation policy that works* (pp. 64–84). Cambridge, MA: MIT Press.

Mathison, S. (Ed.). (2005). *Encyclopedia of evaluation.* Thousand Oaks, CA: Sage.

Mehrota, D. (2006). Applying total quality management in academics. *Six Sigma Magazine.* Retrieved July 23, 2007, from http://www.isixsigma.com/library/content/c020626a.asp

National Institutes of Health. (2006). *NIH roadmap for medical research.* Retrieved July 23, 2007, from http://nihroadmap.nih.gov/initiatives.asp

National Research Council. (1988). *Evaluation of the engineering research centers.* Washington, DC: National Academy Press

National Science Foundation. (1984). *Engineering research centers: How they happened, their purpose, and comments on related programs.* Washington, DC: National Science Foundation.

National Science Foundation. (2005). *National Science Foundation centers.* Retrieved July 24, 2007, from http://www.nsf.gov/pubs/2005/nsf05539/nsf05539.htm

National Science Foundation. (2007). *SRS Info Brief 302: Federal agencies supported by R&D growth over the period FY 1994–2004.* Washington, DC: National Science Foundation.

Newcomer, K. E., Hatry, H. P., & Wholey, J. S. (1994). Meeting the need for practical evaluation approaches: An introduction. In J. S. Wholey, H. P. Hatry, & K. E. Newcomer (Eds.), *Handbook of practical program evaluation* (pp. 1–10). San Francisco: Jossey-Bass.

Organization for Economic Co-Operation and Development. (1987). *Evaluation of research: A selection of current practices.* Paris: OECD.

Patton, M. Q. (1997). *Utilization-focused evaluation: The new century text* (3rd ed.). Thousand Oaks, CA: Sage.

Research centers and services directory (35th ed.). (2006). Farmington Hills, MI: Thomson Gale.

Roessner, D. (2000). *Outcomes and impacts of the state/industry-university cooperative research centers program.* Arlington, VA: SRI International.

Rossi, P. H., Lipsey, M. W., & Freeman, H. E. (2004). *Evaluation: A systematic approach* (7th ed.). Thousand Oaks, CA: Sage.

Ruegg, R., & Feller, I. (2003). *A toolkit for evaluating public R&D investments: Models, methods and findings from ATP's first decade.* Washington, DC: National Institute of Standards and Technology.

Scott, C. (2007). *Compendium of technology breakthroughs of the NSF IUCRC 2007.* Washington, DC: National Science Foundation.

Steenhuis, H., & Gray, D. O. (2005). Strategic decision making in public funded innovative organizations: An exploratory study. *International Journal of Technology Transfer and Commercialisation, 4,* 127–146.

Tornatzky, L. G. (1982, October). *Research on research in the National Science Foundation.* Paper presented at the meeting of the Evaluation Research Society, Baltimore.

Tornatzky, L. G. (2001). Benchmarking university-industry technology transfer: A six-year retrospective. *Journal of Technology Transfer, 26,* 269–277.

Who'd want to work in a team? (2003, 3 July) *Nature, 424,* 1.

DENIS O. GRAY is an alumni distinguished graduate professor in the Psychology in the Public Interest Program, Department of Psychology, North Carolina State University.

Scriven, M., & Coryn, C. L. S. (2008). The logic of research evaluation. In C. L. S. Coryn & M. Scriven (Eds.), *Reforming the evaluation of research. New Directions for Evaluation, 118,* 89–105.

7

The Logic of Research Evaluation

Michael Scriven, Chris L. S. Coryn

Abstract

The authors offer suggestions about logical distinctions often overlooked in the evaluation of research, beginning with a strong plea not to treat technology as applied science, and especially not to treat research in technology as important only if it makes a contribution to scientific knowledge. They argue that the frameworks illustrated in this issue for the evaluation of technology centers and their research are superior to those used for evaluating science centers. Ways to improve the evaluation of research are suggested. © Wiley Periodicals, Inc.

The chapters in this volume exhibit the results of a great deal of experience and insight about the business of evaluating and funding research, and many of those working in this field will read them with interest. Note that "those working in this field" is a larger group than it might appear at first glance, because there are many people working in the field who are not actively engaged in studying the field. Every scientist and administrator of a science center or department is, therefore, included, doing, using, or being responsible for research, and in each role he or she must evaluate it. But "research" is not confined to the sciences. All the humanities do research, as do law and engineering; most intelligent people engaged in running a business are doing research on their own market and operation

and training. Certainly, most of the faculty and administration at institutions of higher education rely on research, and their careers depend on how it is judged. A number of members of the 6,000-strong American Evaluation Association are working on the methodology of evaluating research—hence this volume, to which some of them are contributors (including a couple of its ex-presidents).

How much progress can we expect from focusing the effort as we have here? In particular, how much progress will come from the professional evaluators? One possible answer is in the fall 2007 issue of the *American Journal of Evaluation* (Coryn, Hattie, Scriven, & Hartmann, 2007), which reports on a critical review of 16 countries' efforts to evaluate research, but here we'll try to suggest another answer.

This subject is still in its early days, partly because it's an extremely difficult one. But there do seem to be some ways in which the study of evaluation methodology, based on other fields of evaluation such as program, personnel, and product evaluation, can at least clarify the issues; we'll try to support that view in this essay, by way of commenting on some of the other essays here. Our qualifications are fairly simple; the lead author has worked for some time in evaluation (particularly in such less-populated subareas of it as developing a general theory of evaluation that is supposed to apply to all branches) and done some serious research in a handful of the standard fields of social, biological, medical, and physical sciences; mathematics; philosophy; history; educational research; and technology.

Let's begin at the end of that list. One of the problems with many approaches to the evaluation of research is that they operate as if technology is a branch of science, or perhaps of engineering. But research in technology— or more exactly, in research's counterpart there, R&D, which is something that most governments are very interested in supporting along with the usual kind of scientific research—is not well covered by models from either science or engineering, despite the long-running campaign on the part of those enterprises to convey the impression that they are (or just one of them is) the mother lode of technological excellence. Some of the chapters here scrupulously avoid that mistake, but even Mallon's paper, struggling to create a new paradigm for evaluating software, simulations, and games, gets only one foot outside the box; he still believes (or at least argues from the stance) that work in his areas of interest has to have "scientific research significance" in order to qualify for the kind of funding that governments are dispensing. He says, ". . . Merely producing a new game or simulation or software should not be sufficient to gain research merits and credit. A key question that needs to be answered is, Does it actually constitute scientific research or advancement?" Although this tends to be true of current practice, we'll argue that it is true only by error; it's true only because many of those involved in the usual funding and evaluation process are still confused about technology.

The Autonomy of Technology

To begin with a simple point, it's clear that any serious study of technology must recognize that it provides much of the infrastructure of contemporary art and recreation, not just of science, engineering, medicine, and other conventional kinds of research. Progress in technology occurred, following considerable R&D, when Kazunori Yamauchi created Gran Turismo (GT) in 1997, the most successful computer game of all time. Software inventions are not research-based only when someone invents software that contributes to or includes scientific research, or to educating scientific researchers.

The kind of research behind technology breakthroughs like GT is usually referred to as R&D because there's more to it than we commonly think of as research. For a while, it was often referred to as RDD&E for research, development, dissemination, and evaluation, which is closer to the real package but still misleading. To avoid complications that we have no space to deal with here, we'll generally use the term *reseval* hereafter, to refer to the evaluation of either scientific research or whatever complex of processes is the equivalent in the exploration and creation chain for technology. References to research should be taken as covering the package of cognitive and hands-on processes in both science and technology, and all other domains, that involve systematic invention or discovery followed by a process of systematic, structured, critical analysis and the appropriate kind of development. This conception of research is closely related to what Jordan, Hage, and Mote in this volume—who are highly sensitive to the need to treat technology differently—usefully distinguish as not just R&D but RTD: research, technology, and development.

Doesn't this extended view of research carry the concept too far? Surely, it will even include what every serious painter or novelist does. It doesn't completely exclude them, for there is an element of research in, for example, the serious experiments with representation that the impressionists undertook. But it doesn't put them in competition for state funding, because their topic and product (like those of comparative literature and jurisprudence) don't qualify; art and creative writing do not (or rarely if ever) contribute to explicit testable knowledge about the world or to our body of functional artifacts. Novels and paintings, to take two examples of their products, are not functional artifacts in the common meaning of that phrase, by contrast with the word processor and brushes used to produce them.

On the other hand, despite some reservations from self-styled "hardcore scientists," a correct account of research will include some parts of enterprises, such as taxonomy, measurement theory, mathematics, and the philosophy of science (and perhaps the history of science), for the reason that Einstein gave when he said that part of what he was doing was philosophy; it was reconceptualizing and reorganizing our knowledge about the world. NSF rightly funds those parts.

NEW DIRECTIONS FOR EVALUATION • DOI: 10.1002/ev

The bottom line is that the research behind the invention of GT, or for that matter Technicolor, or the microwave oven, produced large gains in the quality of life for millions of people, and of course, each of them brought in hundreds of millions of dollars to the companies involved and added huge numbers of jobs to payrolls in development, manufacturing, and sales. Mallon's essay certainly argues very well for the case that a radically different model has to be used for evaluating any new artifacts in his category, by contrast with any of those used so far for the evaluation of conventional scientific research contributions. It seems likely that his model is too different and complex to be acceptable in the near future; but anything less than an approximation to it will simply be inadequate in terms of validity and hence utility.

We think his conception of the kind of technology whose development our society needs to be supporting is much too narrow, because it seems clear that even inventing a successful noncomputer game such as Rubik's Cube, or the snowboard, or acrylic artist's paint, or a better toothbrush, also involves serious R&D, even if (a big if) it doesn't involve any scientific breakthroughs. So it's more than just possible that we're an even longer way than he suggests from having a workable solution for evaluating many kinds of socially valuable technological research. Therefore, it's pretty clear that some of the "peer review panels" we need to use in some of these cases must include full voting membership for teenage geeks, such as those who hold most of the world championships in the highly competitive field of international computer gaming. In evaluating research related to more conventional consumer products, representatives from Consumers Union will take their place. All of this makes up one key consideration to keep in mind about further development of reseval: It must avoid treating scientific research as the only kind that's really important. Our lives depend on technology more than they do on science, and they have done so for more than a million years.

Evaluation Keys to Function, Not Just Purpose

In several chapters here, including Mallon's, some other assumptions are made that seem inconsistent with what we have been able to justify in the way of a general logic of evaluation. For example, he and others make the common mistake—for long a dogma in program evaluation, though now rarely argued—of thinking that evaluation approaches should be tied to the *purposes* of the work being evaluated. In fact, once we get beyond the development phase where this is close to the truth, we find that evaluation should be tied only to the *uses or functions* of the evaluand, whether or not they were the intention of its developer; whether ideas or objects, artifacts often turn out to have valuable (and sometimes antisocial) uses the inventor had never imagined. The *success* of research is measured against its purposes (by definition of the word), but its *merit, worth, and significance* are measured against the needs and wants its products serve, whether they are the ones targeted by the purposes or not. Discovering these unanticipated payoffs (or disasters) is an important part of reseval, and it's a part that rarely gets the attention it deserves. For example, as the lead author pointed out in a paper called "Taking Games Seriously" (Scriven, 1987), commercial computer games have long been known to have huge payoffs in remedial physiotherapy and in science education, unequalled in either area by any alternative. Developing these results is neglected partly because people don't fully understand the difference between success and value, and this leads to a serious waste of valuable results. Of course, pharmacological research has long been totally clear that finding side-effects is often more important than finding out whether the drug does what the manufacturer hopes and claims, but we were slow to incorporate the lesson into serious evaluation in other areas.

Activities That Sometimes Pass for Evaluation of Research

To set up a basic framework for evaluating research, which will clarify one or two other problems with approaches common in the reseval field, let's consider the range of activities that pass for, or at least have often been included in, the evaluation of research.

Evaluation of Research in Personnel Evaluation. Because the peer review process is the linchpin of most approaches to research and R&D evaluation, let's start with its use in one of the oldest contexts, personnel evaluation, which we'll then link to the evaluation of research/R&D for the purpose of funding it. Traditionally, one of the worst (that is, most expensive) blunders in the general area of reseval has been to assume that evaluating someone's research *record* is the most important task in evaluating the person's candidacy for a research position (Coryn, 2007). Although it is certainly *an* important part, the best one can say for this is that it can establish a lower bound that must be cleared for appointments to senior positions. If the candidates have never done any good research, then they are not worth considering. Of course, our main task is to evaluate the likelihood that the candidate *will* do good or excellent research in the future, and this difference is absolutely fundamental. Past work can supply one part of the evidence for this, but it is useless unless supplemented by "bridging evidence," that is, evidence that the candidate is going to continue to do work of equal or better quality. This is too often assumed to be an assumption we can reasonably count on, but the size of the investment makes this a blunder. Much of the evidence for the security of the bridge is evidence that there are no cracks in it now, so obviously we need to check for their absence. But university and institute selection committees rarely do any systematic checking of this kind; after all, it's not long since they usually failed to check the legitimacy of claimed academic credentials, or teaching ability even when teaching was a key requirement of the job. The (past to future) "bridge check" should at least look for certain kinds of problem: (1) general burnout (general loss of interest in research) or serious health or personal problems, looking for a drop in productivity or quality in the last year or two, especially with respect to "in press" items; (2) blind alley or boredom problems, looking for recent topic switches (if what you need is further work in the prior area of distinction); (3) dependence on a collaborator who has now gone another way, looking at multiple versus solo authorship record; (4) overcommitment, looking for a major increase in nonresearch activities, including editing, conference convening, administration, media appearances, and (if it's there) double-checking the recent professional work. Beyond those, three other efforts pay off: (5) talking to current or very recent coworkers; (6) asking for, and looking very hard at, "subpublication" materials, for example, content or PowerPoints from recent talks and presentations, book reviews, and lecture notes from current or recent graduate seminars; and (7) using the interview to get into ongoing thought processes with respect to current research efforts. All these indicators can be generalized in doing a monitoring evaluation of a research center or network rather than of an individual.

The Complication of Funding Constraints. When individual research is being evaluated in some kind of funding context other than the narrower kind of personnel issue, such as hiring, promoting, and tenuring, whether by using metrics such as citation indices or by using peer review panels, we must again sharply distinguish between the relative ease of ex post evaluation (the ease is only relative, given the long latency of much research), usually done for accountability, and the massively more hazardous ex ante evaluation, usually for future funding. We tend to wrongly conflate the two, for example, by treating the ex post evaluation as good grounds for continuance of funding, when due diligence requires looking at the seven indicator domains listed here.

There is another and much more serious problem. The evaluation of research required for personnel decisions is either a simple case of grading— that is, we are asking whether the work is good enough to justify appointment at this institution—or, in some cases, a requirement to rank against other candidates, both of which require assessing on a single dimension (merit). Funding for research usually comes from a source that is limited in amount as well as range of interests; hence, the evaluation task has three dimensions: (1) cost must also be considered, (2) relevance to the dimensions of value endorsed by the funder must be considered, and (3) it is virtually always competitive, so ranking on the combination of merit *and* cost *and* relevance is almost always required. These considerations define a different kind of evaluation task, commonly known as portfolio evaluation; it is the defining problem facing investment managers constructing a portfolio of investments. The bad news is that there is nothing like an algorithm for the typical case of portfolio evaluation.

Which is not to say there aren't some favorite suggestions—indeed practices—at least for special cases of portfolio management. Take a simple case: Funding for a research center is cut by 15% under a new government economy drive. How should the cut be distributed across the six main projects, which are of various sizes? There are people who think that a 15% cut across the board would be "fairest," whatever that is supposed to mean in this context. But it's obvious that this action risks cutting some projects below critical mass, whereas others would lose only fat; hence, it cannot be taken seriously. Its main effect might well be proactive, in encouraging submission of inflated budgets the following year, to furnish insulation against further cuts. A bad consequence. Again, one often hears the suggestion that funding should always be on scientific merit, and that we should fund from the top down until we run out of funds. But if the top proposal took all the money available, would it really be optimal to put all one's eggs in one basket? A heart attack for the key investigator on the project could mean nothing to show for more than a year's funding. And what about the strategic effect in terms of loss of young researchers from all the unfunded fields? The simple answers don't work well.

But common practices come too close to these mistakes for comfort. For example, many foundations, both public and private, often dispense funds by asking their peer review panels to rank-order the proposals by merit without regard to cost (the budget pages are often withheld from the panels). This will work reasonably well only under two conditions: (1) the requested amounts are small or very small compared to the amount available and (2) the interests of the foundation or division are closely matched to those of the panelists and applicants. But when we start looking at efforts to fund research or R&D in general—for example, in the 16 countries that centralize most of their funding of these efforts, or in the higher level decisions of foundations with a wide range of interests—then the interests of the country or foundation, the panelists, and the applicants are not collinear, and the second condition fails (and sometimes the first as well) (Coryn, 2007). Given the well-known deficiencies of peer review under the best conditions, and the well-known problems with getting any kind of agreement on interdisciplinary research proposals, it would be a mere leap of fantasy to suggest that panelists who are supposedly expert in judging research merit in a specific field are skilled in judging not just the merit, but also the *comparative cost-effectiveness* of research proposals in a variety of *fields that are competing with their own*. When we toss the incommensurability of technology R&D into this problem, it makes the prospect of an objective solution seem unattainable. This may be the impression many readers will get from some of the chapters in this volume. In what follows, we'll play the devil's advocate for an alternative view to the rather intimidating story from three of them, beginning with Quinlan, Kane, and Trochim on the evaluation of large research initiatives.

Complexity Paralysis. Chapter 5 assembles a number of reactions by the three authors to their experience with several large efforts at NIH research funding of centers or networks. Their reactions are mainly reflections on the complexity and difficulty of evaluating these huge enterprises, with some thoughts about possible approaches, four of which they endorse quite strongly: peer review, concept mapping, program logic modeling, and systems analysis.

In the devil's advocate role, we'll suggest that even though the chapter is indeed a valuable compendium of things to look out for, in this kind of evaluation it is also a demonstration of what one might call complexity paralysis. There's no general design for dealing with these evaluands, not even a framework for designing one, and the impression is left that the whole enterprise is a very uncertain one. There are other reasons for serious disquiet. First, one should surely be uneasy about the exclusive focus they place on "desired outcomes." There is no discussion of undesired outcomes, which are often just as important and sometimes fatal; so they must be earnestly sought, which means doing concept mapping on them as well and following that up with directed search.

Second, they accept the suggestion from another report that one should require external review of research centers "at least every five to seven years." We think that 3 years after start-up and not more than every 2 years after that is more like accountability as most people understand it, and perfectly reasonable. No doubt center researchers, like most academic ones, would like to be left in peace for longer than that, but this is hardly a compelling argument given the public costs involved.

Third, the support for a logic model approach is misguided and involves a huge diversion of resources. Add to this a fourth reason: Most important of all, there is no suggestion at all of a systematic approach to developing and improving a model for doing this kind of evaluation. NIH is supposed to focus on improving research relevant to its mission, and it's obvious that evaluating its work is itself a research problem relevant to its mission. Surely, NIH should be insisting that its evaluation consultants show minimum signs of the standard scientific or technological approach to dealing with complex problems like this one: proposing a testable model that will be systematically trialed and improved.

Outlining an Evaluation Framework

We think one can do better than this kind of approach, on the basis of experience with various large-scale evaluation problems. So, we will push for an alternative approach, which for argument's sake, we will call the Hard-Core Approach (HaCA for short, pronounced, yes, as "hacker," because it is from the world of the technologist and not the scientist, and for those who know that world, hacker is a term of art, not a term of abuse). This is intended to be adequate for ex post or ex ante evaluations, but a slimmer version would be a better instrument for midstream or formative evaluation, and for monitoring purposes.

This approach would be based on a multistep process of a certain kind. Note first that many of the steps listed involve using panels of judges. It is assumed that they will not only be filtered for conflict of interest, correctly interpreted (see Scriven, 1991, for details on this), but also calibrated by running them through some training on carefully chosen examples to resolve major differences, especially those between natural high-raters and low-raters.

1. Take the concept maps, and repeat the exercise so as to identify possible *undesirable* outcomes. Use both results to identify a set of criteria of merit (plus some indicators of their presence) and possible side-effects. Besides outcomes, these lists should also include plenty of process and output criteria.

2. Extract from these maps the tentative weights of the criteria, given there as indications of perceived relative importance according to the stakeholders involved in the concept mapping.

3. Spell out how each of these weights is to be researched for objective reinforcement or modification. Concurrently examine the lists for improvements in their comprehensiveness.

4. Also spell out how each criterion is to be measured, estimated, or judged (that is, identify the indicators for the criteria, including bibliometric as well as judgmental indicators) and the problems with each proposed indicator for doing this, along with alternatives to try when those in the first set fail.

5. Then spell out who is to be committed to the task of finding *further unanticipated or undesirable* consequences, processes, and indicators, and how they are to find them.

6. Run measures on each directly measurable dimension and all indicators, synthesize the results to get a performance score on each dimension, and normalize them to a 100-point scale where quantitative measures are being used (and to regions on a scale of merit when qualitative measures are involved). Add extensive notes about extenuating, moderating, or facilitating circumstances, including personal, internal, systemic, environmental, or political factors; indicate their probable influence, with estimates of amount or at least direction.

7. Place bars on the performance scales to locate *absolute* minimum acceptable performance, and document the reasoning.

8. Place markers on each scale to indicate minimum cutting scores for Exceptional, Good, Satisfactory, Marginal, and Unacceptable, or just for these distinctions in their own right if using qualitative measures, with appropriate documentation for their location.

9. Plot the results as a bar graph with the bar widths representing the weighting of each dimension. This process will yield a preliminary

"profile" for each center evaluated, an extremely useful tool for indicating need for improvement or grounds for congratulation. It is good minimalist methodology to avoid trying to reduce this to a one-dimensional rating unless ranking the centers is critical.

10. If ranking is necessary (that is, to guide a competitive decision about refunding), redraw the profiles using only common dimensions (life-years saved, quality of life increase, accident reduction, major and minor discoveries, research productivity, and so on). Note: the best way to develop the common elements into what we'll call "comparison profiles" is probably to involve some redefinition of important dimensions, which may require reconfirmation with earlier advisers. Now use the areas under the comparison profiles as the measure of merit, because that area represents the product of the achievements and their weights for importance. This brings us to the rest of the R&D approach.

11. Run the appropriate version of this model on three or four volunteer centers or networks, two with similar missions and one or two with entirely different missions. Start discussing its validity and utility (and cost) with all interested parties in each of them; with other key stakeholders, especially those at the receiving end of the (typically required) technology transfer and educational or training efforts; and with two or three external evaluators with relevant experience who are asked to do one-day critiques.

12. Modify the procedures in light of this feedback, and show the result to other centers, funders, and stakeholders for their feedback.

13. Have the product evaluated by an evaluator who is highly trained at cost analysis, in order to get a grip on the first half of a cost-effectiveness evaluation of your approach.

14. Repeat this cycle as often as you repeat use of the gradually improving model, revising accordingly. In the second and later rounds, add a small annex aimed at detecting results from the evaluation approach itself.

15. After two cycles, at most, use an external evaluation panel to do an evaluation of the cost-effectiveness and cost-benefit of the HaCA model.

Ah, yes, but for that we'll need to know the benefits from the *centers*. We can't determine whether *they* were worth what they cost unless we can show that the outcomes we've been cataloging are due to the centers; because their staff is (and was, before the centers came into existence) a highly productive group, they might have done all this without the huge additional cost of the centers. More on this below.

What about the logic model? Logic models are simply theories about how the evaluand works, and though it would sure be nice to have one (or more), the evaluator certainly doesn't need them and is not the best source of them.

What about systems approaches? We've just done one; note step 6. Systems approaches are what make us look beyond the neighborhood for the action, and we've been doing that. But they have risks of bogging down in the awesome complexity they uncover, and we've tried to avoid those. The HaCA model treats evaluation as a specific, limited part of the scientific enterprise and the technological enterprise, done to the extent that this can be done, as it has always been done in science and technology. Analytical models abstract from systems and learn from systems thinking; they don't simply report on systems. Evaluation is not an add-on from another universe of discourse; it's just an analytical tool that applies the usual rules to analysis.

The reader might ask, Because this is a volume about the evaluation of research, why are the editors writing so much about evaluation design? Reseval involves development of tools for analysis, so we must be able to show that our design embodies good R&D principles that govern tool development. If the *evaluation* part of the evaluation of research doesn't follow the rules of good research and development, researchers would have no reason to take it seriously.

Applying the Framework.   Let's see how the HaCA approach, as developed so far, applies to some of the other interesting chapters in this volume. Then, we'll come back to the biggest challenge: the causation problem.

First, we'll look at Gray's excellent paper, which deals with evaluation in the context of technology transfer and technology development. Interestingly enough, in chapter, on exactly the topic just discussed, we find much of the HaCA point of view. For example, Gray clearly endorses the distinction between ex ante research proposal evaluation and ex ante portfolio evaluation. He stresses that for the latter, one has to use at least some review committee members—or possibly a separate level of review—who are looking at investment criteria and not just quality criteria, and who have relevant expertise for such appraisals. He tends to regard this as "modified peer-review"—which is true, but we'd describe it as a logically different task (portfolio versus performance evaluation), for which we can also use peer review. Additionally, he notes the usual weakness on the causal question (". . . few of these studies have included comparison to defensible control or comparison groups, or even to accepted objective norms"). But his particular interest is in improving use of evaluation to assist program managers, and his favored model is quite like a smaller version of the HaCA model outlined here, with a strong emphasis on focusing its findings for improvement. Its use of an onsite evaluator, reporting both to the center director and the national evaluation team, is a distinctive and sensible feature aimed at this focus, though Gray realizes the problems of conflict of interest that result, and the problem of "questionnaire fatigue" from an active and ever-present evaluator. The evaluator's obligation to do exit interviews with consortium partners who resign is a good example of the more general duty to follow up on bad outcomes, as described in HaCA step 5. There are a few key things missing in this model, compared to HaCA, and its users should at least try employing evaluators instead of social scientists as the internal evaluators.

Reseval in Technology Sets the Standard. The main problem that we see with the IUCRC effort follows from the absence of problems with it. It has been running with good results for a quarter century, at a longitudinal total of 110 centers, at low cost, and surely generating powerful evidence of merit. So, why is it not being used in all the other contexts our authors here are writing about? They miss half the points embodied in it, and though they are happily generalizing from it (for example, from a health context to all scientific research programs), apparently it didn't occur to them to generalize from a technology-related program to an NIH program. Or did they just not know about it? Or, perhaps their NIH liaison staff didn't know about it, or thought it inappropriate to use a technology model in a science context. These explanations look very like symptoms of the usual status problem we noted earlier: treating science as the core subject and technology as simply a spin-off. The fundamental point might be put by saying that research evaluation in technology is the more general process; research in science is a special case, involving just one or two of the components in technology reseval.

Necessary and Unnecessary Complications. The alternatives to using something like the IUCRC or HaCA model are illustrated in the chapters from Japan and the group most strongly advocating a theory-based approach, led by Jordan. They offer their own, heavily experience-based and entirely different approaches to the task here. But each runs into difficulties of its own. There are two problems with the Japanese approach, essentially based on hierarchies of review panels. First, its great complexity creates a major difficulty for synthesizing the component evaluations repeatably and defensibly. Second, because it is built on panel ratings, the problem of avoiding bias and lack of calibration becomes critical in the choice and use of panel members and is apparently not treated as central. On the other hand, the approach of Jordan and colleagues, which shares a high degree of complexity, faces up to it better than the Japanese approach but runs into commitment to a theory-based approach, which essentially means it eventually bites off more than anyone can chew. It's now time to say a bit more about this and about the related "attribution" problem: the daunting problem of attributing a causal role to the big science approach of the centers and networks.

The Theory-Based Approach to Evaluation. Evaluation clients usually want, and sometimes require, that the evaluator explain how the evaluand brings about its results, or fails to bring them about. This is because (1) it would certainly be useful for clients to have such an account as an aid to management and development and (2) they have a limited understanding of the nature of evaluation and think this is just an option for the evaluator that they wish to reinforce.

However, what professional evaluation literally means is systematic and well-supported determination of the merit, worth, or significance of whatever is being evaluated, which has absolutely nothing to do with explaining

NEW DIRECTIONS FOR EVALUATION • DOI: 10.1002/ev

how or why it works or fails to work. The FDA approach can and has evaluated hundreds of medicines (and for that matter it can be used to evaluate snake oil and faith-healing)—which is to say we have determined whether, when, how well, and for whom they work, but without having the slightest idea why they do or don't work. We can evaluate new approaches to addiction or crime prevention without deciding which component in them is doing the work, let alone what underlying theory explains the role of all the components. After all, no one has such a theory yet, so why should one imagine that the evaluator can come up with one where the specialists in the field have not yet been successful in doing so?

We need to be clear that doing the evaluation job saves lives and careers and pain and suffering, and a waste of resources, even if it doesn't answer many interesting and scientifically appropriate questions. Advice to clients: don't load the evaluator with the job of the specialist scientist, or you will often not get an answer to the evaluation question (or you'll get a weak answer to it) because of the diversion of time and resources away from getting a full and well-supported answer. Of course, the evaluator often gets lucky and the explanation of success or failure becomes obvious in the course of the evaluation. But this doesn't always happen, and the client should settle for getting what the evaluator *can* do; it's hard enough in itself. So, although the efforts at a general theory of collaborative research produced or reviewed by Jordan, Hage, and Mote are interesting and helpful steps toward this important goal, they are not necessary for evaluating these approaches; nor are they sufficient either, and they are expensive and diversionary. Plenty of evaluators disagree with this view, but it's clear the straight and narrow path is hard enough, and important enough, so one should be happy to find a logical basis for arguing that the rest is someone else's job.

Mention of the evaluation task being hard enough brings us to the attribution problem.

Does the Big Science Approach Pay off? In the horse-racing game, it's easy to distinguish between punters (aka betters) and trainers. The punter's game is pure prediction, and within limits the predictions don't affect the outcome; the trainer's game is to change the outcomes. In business, the line between types of player is harder to draw. Some investors are entirely remote, some turn up at the stockholders' meetings and vote, and some tell the board of directors to do something different. In both fields, it's not too hard to tell whether the activists had a good or bad effect; the horses trained by a good trainer do much better than they did before being moved to his stable, and the company's stock takes off after the board does what the big investor tells them to do. In funding science and technology, the funding agencies are highly proactive, but it's extremely hard to tell whether their actions produce an improvement. Any kind of control group is absurd, and comparison groups that are reasonably comparable are not to be found. The big hope, one might suppose, is a rash of Nobel prizes in the NIH or NSF centers. But the center directors might just be clever punters; they might have just picked and corralled the researchers that were going to do well anyway. We'll suggest a three-pronged approach as the best we can do; but it's not going to give conclusive results in many cases, only in some.

The first two of these components rely on a particular variation of the interrupted time series quasi-experimental design that we'll call the *progression discontinuity* (PD) design (by analogy with regression discontinuity). In the first investigation, the macro prong, the PD approach uses panels of experts from Europe, Asia, and South America who have been working in the field since well before creation of the center under evaluation. The panel is convened (electronically, with video and voice) for the first time about 3 to 4 years after the center starts up, and panel members are asked to take a day to discuss and judge whether, in their view, there has been significant acceleration in the rate or excellence of the production of significant or high-quality research (and products, if we are looking at a technology center) in the United States since the center was created. The panel is reconvened about 3 years later and asked the same question. Additionally, it is asked to treat this as a research problem, on which some members may wish to do further investigation, for which a small amount of funding will be available.

The bias problem here, as in the other panel-based component, is serious: those panelists who favor big centers will be inclined to see successes, and those who oppose them the reverse. The panel should be midsized for credibility and if possible balanced between these two groups and a group of those with no known stand on the issue. There also needs to be some discussion in the panel of whether any other events in the field might have had this effect; they can approach this by reflecting on the research trajectory in their own regions. The assumptions on which this approach rests are fairly obvious, but something like this may be the only way to cover one aspect of any significant change due to the center.

The meso-level prong involves doing the same kind of trajectory analysis—looking for PDs—at the individual level in the career output of the leading scientists or technologists in the center, a group that should include at least 90% of those on the payroll for 2 years or more at the time of the review, which should be 3 years after start-up and usually every 2 years thereafter. In this case, we can use U.S. and Canadian panelists. The key point here is that a discontinuity in the level of research production— quality or quantity—is the sign that the center paid off, not just a high or slightly increasing level in these respects (maturation will produce the latter).

The micro-level approach is different. Let's call it "support net analysis" (SNA). It employs a combination of interviews and focus groups targeting the center's initial (and other senior) staff and aims to focus self-reports and participant observer reports on this question: Can the researchers in the centers point to specific cases or a balance of evidence from their experience that either the distinctive structure, infrastructure, or personnel composition of the center, by contrast with a normal department or institute within a department, significantly assisted (or, of course, hindered) their work? Here, a comparison run of the same structured interviewing and focus group meetings will be done with researchers of approximately the same reputation, though not necessarily in the same field, who by choice or otherwise did not join a center. The point of this is a commonsense one: If the best researchers in the field report a major difference in the amount of what they believe to be valuable input, or in a net reduction of frustrations (that is, net of a possibly increased number of meetings and so on) brought about by the center arrangement, and if those in centers judge that their own work has improved accordingly, it's plausible to infer that this did indeed have some benefits for their work, at least as long as the macro- and meso-level approaches do not indicate the contrary.

Panel Selections for Ex Ante Evaluation of Research Funding. It's tough enough to do ex ante evaluation of a researcher for an appointment, the personnel evaluation problem. It's even harder to do ex ante evaluation of a group of proposals for funding, the task faced by every funder. This is portfolio evaluation, and to conclude this chapter, we're going to make two suggestions about panel management for this, in addition to the stress on calibration and "lightweight" conflict of interest filtering already mentioned. First, just as rating technological research requires recruiting people such as computer gamers as judges, rating portfolios requires getting truly expert portfolio managers on the panels. This means enlisting some *senior* managers at *successful* investment funds. Since this group are paid salaries in the high millions per annum, an appeal to national interest and perhaps prestige will be the key. But they demonstrably have the balancing skills required for good investment where cost is a major constraint, and they are used to evaluating the expertise of those advising them on the quality of content. We have to assume we can learn from them.

Second, we'll mention the apparent need to supply an antidote to the tendency of panels to undersupport "new-paradigm proposals. Because most panelists are by definition doing "within-paradigm" research, they probably have—we should suppose—a tendency to favor such proposals. It seems to be a consensus amongst Nobelers, who frequently discuss this issue when they get together as they quite often do, that currently funded research is badly skewed against radical innovations; good research methods require that we should consider trial implementation of corrective strategies.

One remedy that has been kicked around is the "set-aside" approach. Ask the panelists for ratings of 90% (or 95%) of the available funding in the usual way. For the remaining 5 or 10%, there are two possibilities. First, ask some Nobel-level innovators to come in as panelists for this task only (they won't usually come in for the pro bono heavy lifting involved in ranking all the entries). Less desirably, ask the original panel to furnish a parallel rating of all the proposals on another basis, say, for maximum pay-off if they are successful to the field or to society, regardless of whether they are rated as likely to be successful, with the only constraints being the technical qualifications of the principal investigator(s) and the adequacy of any required infrastructure. When the resulting recommendations go to the panel that considers the costs, enormously expensive proposals can be trimmed if possible, or weighted down by their cost in an appropriate way; this will discourage submitting certain kinds of fantasies (time travel using large specially built neutrino accelerators).

Conclusion

The main themes of these comments have been that:

1. There is a fundamental logical and hence methodological divide among several kinds of evaluation that are involved in the general field of "research evaluation," particularly the differences between ex ante (aka predictive) and ex post (aka retrospective) evaluation, and between performance (aka achievement) or personnel evaluation and portfolio evaluation.

2. The complex activity involving research that occurs in technological progress requires a more complex treatment on the part of evaluators than the more familiar scientific research.

3. Both can be handled by an appropriately complex evaluation framework already well started in the case of technology.

4. Development of that framework must be treated as a typical task in the technology of tool development, which is, regrettably, not yet being done or seriously considered in the science domain.

5. Evaluating big-science research operations is a categorically different enterprise from explaining how it does or does not work, and including the explanation task with the evaluation task adds a further degree of complexity we are nowhere near handling.

6. The question of whether big-science approaches pay-off can be answered through a systematic approach, but only if the gains are large and the budget substantial.

7. A number of ways are suggested in which we need to improve the basic building blocks in reseval, in, for example, selecting senior research personnel, searching for side-effects, selecting and calibrating peer review panels, and evaluating radical research proposals.

References

Coryn, C. L. S. (2007). *Evaluation of researchers and their research: Toward making the implicit explicit.* Unpublished doctoral dissertation, Western Michigan University, Kalamazoo.

Coryn, C. L. S., Hattie, J. A., Scriven, M., & Hartmann, D. J. (2007). Models and mechanisms for evaluating government-funded research: An international comparison. *American Journal of Evaluation, 28*(4), 437–457.

Scriven. M. (1987). *Taking games seriously*. Retrieved September 13, 2007, from http://homepages.wmich.edu/~mscriven/

Scriven, M. (1991). *Evaluation thesaurus* (4th ed.). Thousand Oaks, CA: Sage.

MICHAEL SCRIVEN *is a professor of psychology teaching evaluation in the School of Behavioral and Organizational Sciences, Claremont Graduate University.*

CHRIS L. S. CORYN *is an assistant professor and director of the Interdisciplinary Ph.D. Program in Evaluation at The Evaluation Center, Western Michigan University.*

NEW DIRECTIONS FOR EVALUATION • DOI: 10.1002/ev

INDEX

NEW DIRECTIONS FOR EVALUATION
Order Form

SUBSCRIPTIONS AND SINGLE ISSUES

DISCOUNTED BACK ISSUES:

Use this form to receive **20% off** all back issues of New Directions for Evaluation. All single issues priced at **$21.60** (normally $29.00)

TITLE	ISSUE NO.	ISBN

Call 888-378-2537 or see mailing instructions below. When calling, mention the promotional code, JB7ND, to receive your discount.

SUBSCRIPTIONS: *(1 year, 4 issues)*

☐ New Order   ☐ Renewal

U.S.	☐ Individual: $85	☐ Institutional: $215
Canada/Mexico	☐ Individual: $85	☐ Institutional: $255
All Others	☐ Individual: $109	☐ Institutional: $289

Call 888-378-2537 or see mailing and pricing instructions below. Online subscriptions are available at www.interscience.wiley.com.

Copy or detach page and send to:
John Wiley & Sons, Journals Dept, 5th Floor
989 Market Street, San Francisco, CA 94103-1741

Order Form can also be faxed to: 888-481-2665

Issue/Subscription Amount: $ _____
Shipping Amount: $ _____
(for single issues only—subscription prices include shipping)
Total Amount: $ _____

SHIPPING CHARGES:

SURFACE	Domestic	Canadian
First Item	$5.00	$6.00
Each Add'l Item	$3.00	$1.50

(No sales tax for U.S. subscriptions. Canadian residents, add GST for subscription orders. Individual rate subscriptions must be paid by personal check or credit card. Individual rate subscriptions may not be resold as library copies.)

☐ Payment enclosed (U.S. check or money order only. All payments must be in U.S. dollars.)

☐ VISA   ☐ MC   ☐ Amex # _____ Exp. Date _____

Card Holder Name _____ Card Issue # _____

Signature _____ Day Phone _____

☐ Bill Me (U.S. institutional orders only. Purchase order required.)

Purchase order # _____
Federal Tax ID13559302   GST 89102 8052

Name _____

Address _____

Phone _____ E-mail _____

JB7ND

NEW DIRECTIONS FOR EVALUATION
IS NOW AVAILABLE ONLINE AT WILEY INTERSCIENCE

What is Wiley InterScience?

Wiley InterScience is the dynamic online content service from John Wiley & Sons delivering the full text of over 300 leading scientific, technical, medical, and professional journals, plus major reference works, the acclaimed Current Protocols laboratory manuals, and even the full text of select Wiley print books online.

What are some special features of Wiley InterScience?

Wiley Interscience Alerts is a service that delivers table of contents via e-mail for any journal available on Wiley InterScience as soon as a new issue is published online.
Early View is Wiley's exclusive service presenting individual articles online as soon as they are ready, even before the release of the compiled print issue. These articles are complete, peer-reviewed, and citable.
CrossRef is the innovative multi-publisher reference linking system enabling readers to move seamlessly from a reference in a journal article to the cited publication, typically located on a different server and published by a different publisher.

How can I access Wiley InterScience?

Visit http://www.interscience.wiley.com.

Guest Users can browse Wiley InterScience for unrestricted access to journal Tables of Contents and Article Abstracts, or use the powerful search engine.
Registered Users are provided with a *Personal Home Page* to store and manage customized alerts, searches, and links to favorite journals and articles. Additionally, Registered Users can view free Online Sample Issues and preview selected material from major reference works.
Licensed Customers are entitled to access full-text journal articles in PDF, with select journals also offering full-text HTML.

How do I become an Authorized User?

Authorized Users are individuals authorized by a paying Customer to have access to the journals in Wiley InterScience. For example, a University that subscribes to Wiley journals is considered to be the Customer.
Faculty, staff and students authorized by the University to have access to those journals in Wiley InterScience are Authorized Users. Users should contact their Library for information on which Wiley journals they have access to in Wiley InterScience.

ASK YOUR INSTITUTION ABOUT WILEY INTERSCIENCE TODAY!

Complete online access for your institution

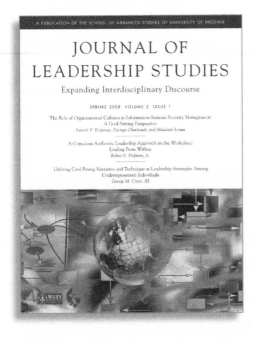

Register for complimentary online access to *Journal of Leadership Studies* today!